BEYOND
ACCEPTANCE

Carolyn Welch Griffin

Marian J. Wirth

and Arthur G. Wirth

Foreword by
Adele Starr

Introduction by
Brian McNaught

■

BEYOND
ACCEPTANCE

■

Parents of Lesbians

and Gays Talk About

Their Experiences

(Revised and

Updated Edition)

St. Martin's Griffin ■ New York

Design by Songhee Kim

Library of Congress Cataloging-in-Publication
Data

Griffin, Carolyn Welch
    Beyond acceptance: parents of lesbians
and gays talk about their experiences/by
Carolyn Welch Griffin, Marian J. Wirth, &
Arthur G. Wirth; foreword by Adele Starr;
introduction by Brian McNaught.— Rev.
and updated ed., 1st ed.
        p. cm.
    Includes bibliographical references and
index.
    ISBN 0-312-16781-4
    1.   Homosexuality — United   States.
2. Lesbians—United States—Family relationships. 3. Gay men—United States—
Family relationships. 4. Parents of gays—
United States. 5. Parent and child—United
States. I. Wirth, Marian Jenks. II. Wirth,
Arthur G. III. Title.
HQ76.3.U5G75   1996
306.874—dc20   96-22366
                                CIP

10   9   8   7   6   5   4   3   2

■

We were learners. We learned most from our own gay children, our families, and from the parents who let us record their words. Their willingness to share recollections of the journey that took them to acceptance and beyond made it possible for us to bring this book into being.

CONTENTS

ACKNOWLEDGMENTS

We wish to acknowledge permission from the following publishers to quote from copyrighted materials cited in the text: Dignity, Inc.; Friends Book Center; The Pilgrim Press; Sage Publications, Inc.; and Redwood Records. We would also like to thank Methodist Bishop Melvin Wheatley (ret.), who permitted us to quote from an address he delivered.

Many people helped and encouraged us in various stages of the writing. We owe a special debt of gratitude to Robin Griffin, who typed endless transcripts of interviews; to Becky Torstrick for her care and accuracy in preparing the final draft of the first edition, and to Jim Thomas for his insightful editorial advice.

We wish to express our thanks to John Pingree for his patience in deciphering our handwriting and for his precision in typing the many drafts of this revised edition.

■

FOREWORD

■

by ADELE STARR

I t is more than twenty years since parents of gay and lesbian children began meeting in groups across the nation. When we first got together, it was for the purpose of bringing support and comfort to one another. We told our family histories and shared our feelings and experiences. What evolved was the realization that our gay sons and lesbian daughters were not a problem; that the problem was a very misinformed society.

Our observations have helped us to understand gay persons. We have learned that for up to 10 percent of the population it is natural to be attracted to the same sex; that there really is no choice in one's sexuality; and that there is no pattern to the kind of family that has a gay child. The love we had for our children sustained us while we learned.

Today there are more than four hundred parent groups and affiliates in the United States plus another ten in foreign countries. And more are in formation. Because our children are victims of a great deal of misinformation, we are trying to change attitudes toward them by speaking out and by sharing with you—our community-at-large—what we have learned.

This is what the authors of *Beyond Acceptance* have accomplished. They have invited you into their lives through interviews with parents and others in their local parent group, through their rap and discussion meetings, and by sharing their thoughts and experiences. They have written about their group so you can observe the stages that so many of us parents have gone through.

Each parent group is unique, yet each is the same. The group represented in this book is in the heartland of America. It speaks for all of us. It gets to the heart of the parents' movement.

When I first became involved twenty years ago, I had hopes that we would put ourselves out of business in a few years. It is still my hope, but as long as we are needed we will be available. That's for sure!

> *Adele Starr,* Past President
> Parents, Families and Friends
> of Lesbians and Gays (National)

EDITOR'S NOTE: Jeanne and Jules Manford started the first group of Parents, Families and Friends of Lesbians and Gays (Parents FLAG or P-FLAG) in 1973 in New York City. Adele and Larry Starr and colleagues started the Los Angeles group in 1976. Adele Starr was the first president of the national P-FLAG, which incorporated in 1981. Her term as president ran from 1981 to 1987.

■

INTRODUCTION

■

by BRIAN McNAUGHT

For New Year's Eve, 1990, my partner, Ray, and I flew to Sarasota for what we knew would be Mom's last holiday celebration. There we joined the folks in the ritual of watching the televised descent of the ball in Times Square and we greeted the new year with cheers, hugs, and kisses.

Mom died of cancer the following spring. Dad followed her four years later after suffering a heart attack. And though I miss them both enormously, I live without doubt that they both loved me and were very proud of me. Sadly, all gay people cannot say the same.

Frequently when I speak publicly about homosexuality, I will notice men and women in the audience crying silently as they hear me say I have no unfinished business with my folks. Afterward they will often identify themselves as either the closeted gay child of a parent who has died or the parent of a deceased gay child who never heard their parent say, "I love you just the way you are."

This wonderful book is designed to eliminate such tears of regret. It belongs in the hands of every parent, family member, and friend who knows or suspects someone they love is gay and in the hands of every gay person who is about to share his or her beautiful though often unsettling secret. *Beyond Acceptance,* now updated to reflect important breakthroughs in science and in public perceptions, provides a clear and reliable road map for those who seek mutual understanding and respect between straight parents and gay children.

I wish my folks had had access to this book in 1974. Though they ultimately made it through the journey, *Beyond Acceptance* would have comforted them early in the process by affirming their feelings. It would have answered their many questions with an authority I could not have, and led them patiently, gently, and safely to new levels of understanding and perhaps involvement.

When I came out to them at age twenty-six, my dear mother wept out of fear of what the world would do to me and out of shame that she had failed. Dad's approach was more hopeful. He assured me that I had a hormone imbalance I would outgrow. Regrettably, they had to struggle with their feelings in a vacuum, void of peer support or accurate information. The same would not be true today.

As I read these poignant reflections by the parents of other gay people, I hear Mom and Dad as they might have sounded confiding to a friend. Their initial fear, hurt, denial, anger, alienation, and shame, among other feelings, are all here. One of the great strengths of this book is its testimonies by real people who have made the journey through these emotions. Parents of gay people who are confused and in pain will be comforted and encouraged by the "chats" they can have with these anonymous new friends.

Once secure in the assurance they are not alone in their feelings, parents of gay people are then freed to think more clearly about their situation and to seek answers to their many questions. Most parents will be as confused by the subject of homosexuality as gay people are initially. That lack of familiarity with the topic often leads to fear. And, as most people would agree, the best antidote to fear is factual information and exposure.

Beyond Acceptance does a fine job in presenting accurate information about homosexuality, addressing such concerns as "Is it a choice?" and "Can it be changed?" Readers will find all of their questions answered or will be referred to an extensive list of reliable resources.

Beyond the facts, what separates this book from others with the same message is the unique voice of the messenger. Though my parents respected me, it was far more effective for them to eventually hear from a heterosexual peer than from me that I made no choice in being gay. In these pages, heterosexual parents share with other heterosexual parents information they found trustworthy and helpful.

Once equipped with accurate information, many parents are then ready to take the next step forward and embrace without fear their gay child and to build with him or her a new relationship based upon honesty. No more changed pronouns. No more pretending not to see. No more putting safe distance between one another. It is an incredibly beautiful thing to witness.

Sometimes this new acceptance of the gay child manifests itself in small ways, like phone calls that end with "Give our love to Ray." And sometimes it is seen in more dramatic ways as parents, family, and friends go beyond acceptance and involve themselves in the struggle of the gay person for safety and equity in society.

Some parents join Parents, Families and Friends of Lesbians and Gays (P-FLAG). Some hold signs in gay pride marches that read, "I love my gay child." Some write wonderful books in order to share their experiences and insights with others.

What parents who go beyond acceptance don't do is weep in regret for a lost relationship with a gay child.

■

PREFACE

■

Τhis is a story from parents of lesbian and gay children. More specifically, it is a report of the experiences of twenty-three parents who worked together over a period of years in a self-help organization called Parents, Families and Friends of Lesbians and Gays (Parents FLAG).* The authors and others in the group have wrestled with the personal and cultural implications of the fact that we are parents of gay or lesbian adult children. We have been moved by the varieties of pain that

*Parents FLAG is a national network of scores of self-help groups from all parts of the United States. See Appendix.

we and our children have suffered. We have been equally moved by the varieties of growth that emerged as, together, we confronted our common experience. Our need to report grew out of our own awareness of changes taking place in us personally and in others in the group.

Because our society still rejects gay people, most parents of lesbians and gays will experience some of the varieties of pain we have known. We realize that parents who discover that someone in their family is gay often feel terribly isolated. It can be a great relief to learn that they are not alone.

We also want to share the varieties of personal and family growth that we have seen in our group. We make no claims for smooth transition from pain to enlightenment, but we know that our transformations have been real. Our changes are not fixed; we are very much aware that we too are "in process."

The group members interviewed were white, middle-class Americans from a large Midwestern metropolitan area. They were from widely differing vocational, educational, and religious backgrounds, with ages ranging from forty to eighty.

As in any self-help group, members of Parents FLAG join for varying periods of time. Our direct quotes are based on interviews with parents who joined the group and stayed in for a considerable length of time. In this sense, the group we interviewed was self-selected. Names and places have been changed to preserve privacy. We are not social scientists, but have read many studies about gay people in America. Our understanding has been significantly broadened by our reading as well as by our experiences. We draw on both in commenting on what we have learned that may be helpful to other parents of lesbian or gay children.

On Terminology

Homosexuality is a varied and complex phenomenon. There are, for example, many people who have experienced homosexual incidents. These have not affected their heterosexual orientation. There are others who are bisexual. In this book, our remarks refer primarily to that category of sexuality which characterizes most of the gay or lesbian children of parents in our group. Our children's orientation is primarily or exclusively homosexual. They have no more inclination or ability to change their sexual orientation than do those of us who are exclusively heterosexual.

As we consider the terms *homosexual* or *gay* to be interchangeable, a brief comment on the term *gay* is in order. There seems to be no single, simple account of its origins. Gay people themselves prefer to be called lesbian or gay rather than homosexual. To many gay people the word *homosexual* emphasizes only the sexual aspect of their lives, while *lesbian* or *gay* refers to the entire range of their human relationships. It also indicates the positive feelings they have about their sexual orientation. Because *homosexual* is a word in general usage, however, we will from time to time use it as an alternative to *gay*. Many women in the gay community prefer to be called *lesbian*, therefore, we will often use the term *gay men and lesbians,* although we will use *gay* occasionally as the umbrella term.

Heterosexism is a word that has moved into common usage. Like the words *racism, sexism, ageism,* or *classism,* it refers to the idea that one group—in this case heterosexuals—is superior and only that group is truly acceptable. With all of these terms there is an implicit requirement by the "superior" group that those in the secondary group "stay in their place." They should not have the same privileges or rights. They should not in any way disturb those in power, nor challenge the written or unwritten rules. If they do, the majority feels justified in punishing and ostracizing those who are different.

Another word that we use is *homophobia*. This word comes from George Weinberg's book *Society and the Healthy Homosexual.* It means an irrational and excessive fear of lesbians and gay men that often leads to hate and even violence. Homophobia is pervasive throughout our culture, and it is this fear that must be countered. We hope this book will make a contribution to removing the fear.

Carolyn Welch Griffin
Marian J. Wirth
Arthur G. Wirth

BEYOND
ACCEPTANCE

*As the truth replaces fear and
superstition, attitudes are
changing. In the meantime,
don't let society rob you of your
special child.*[1]

ONE

FINDING OUT

The moment when our children chose to tell us of their homosexuality was a moment of shock and pain. Our lives were placed on a different course. Years do not erase the details of the day. We recall the weather, the time of day, the room, our thoughts, and, most of all, our feelings. It was a moment that marked the beginning of a journey through a powerful grief.

It happened on a Sunday morning—a sunny day in February. We were still in bed when Craig came into the room and said, "I have something I want to tell you."

He sat at the foot of the bed, crossed his arms, and I thought, "Oh my God." Then he said, "I can't lie to you anymore. I'm gay."

The words made my ears ring. We argued, and there was some uproar. I begged him not to act on it, but he already had. It was a bad scene for a while. Later, after I quieted down, I had a feeling that was about the same as when somebody dies. For a long time I went around with a lump in my throat.

■

We were all sitting around our daughter's living room, with a Christmas tree in the corner—a regular family gathering. Chris said he had something to tell us, and then he hemmed and hawed for what seemed like five minutes. He said things like "I don't know how to tell you this," and "This may be hard to hear."

If I had it to do over again, I would have helped him by saying, "Are you trying to tell us you're gay?" But at that time, I didn't consciously admit to myself that I had any idea of what was coming. I think I did know, down deep somewhere, but I just wanted to postpone what I perceived as difficult news, if even for a few minutes.

Finally, Chris said something about the fact that he was attracted to men. Since Jack and I had had some suspicions in the past because Chris hadn't dated, it wasn't a complete shock.

I remember thinking, "Well, this is it. The die is cast, and what we feared has come to pass." I was disappointed, but the full effect didn't hit me until later.

I knew I should support Chris's decision, and I did. I just put all the worries about my feelings on hold.

■

Our daughter sent my wife and me a letter to tell us. She said she chose this method because she wanted to think out her thoughts very carefully. I think she told us very diplomatically. She wrote that being a lesbian was important in her life and that she had to share it with us. She then asked for our response.

My wife and I felt like our world had come to an end. We hit the depths of our emotions. We had guilt feelings and thought that everything we had done with our children was wrong. For a brief time, we even thought about mutual suicide.

Nancy and Paul had a special problem with their son, Tim, who is totally deaf. Both parents had spent long hours helping with Tim's education. They are a close and caring family.

Nancy: *When we first found out, it was very traumatic.*

Paul: *Tim had been having a terrible time emotionally. The deaf are very emotional people anyway, because they have a harder time expressing themselves than do hearing persons. He had been throwing temper tantrums.*

Nancy: *We had at least a year and a half that was rough before we found out.*

Paul: *He didn't know how to cope with it. He didn't know how to tell us.*

Nancy: *We didn't know what to do. We were walking on eggs, trying not to say anything wrong because he was so keyed up. We found out later he had discussed being gay with his older brother, who told him it was just a phase. That didn't help, and finally he had even thought of killing himself.*

Paul: *We weren't fighting him. We were trying to help him. But we didn't know how to protect him. We had no idea that he was so upset because he was gay.*

Nancy: *We told him we were trying to help him cope with what was bothering him. He kept saying, "You don't understand. You just don't understand." I said, "No, we don't understand you, but we're trying to."*

Paul: *Then one morning about three o'clock, he woke us up and told us his truck had been stolen. It was a fancy pickup truck, and he told us it had been taken on the east side—a bar area. Boy, did he hate to tell us about that robbery. I said, "My God, what were you doing over on the east side? You know you're not supposed to be over there!" I went back to bed, because I was tired and a bit disgusted.*

Nancy: *Tim and I stayed up and were sitting at the kitchen table. And I said, "Tim, I just can't imagine your being stupid enough to be over there on the east side. You know what goes on over there."*

Then he looked at me and said, "I'm gay. That's why I was there."

And with that I said, "I knew something was wrong, but I didn't know what. I thought you were over there fooling around with whores."

Right away we started talking. He said, "I don't want to be that way, Mother, but I am."

I said, "Who got to you?"

He said, "Nobody."

I said, "Don't tell me that. I know somebody got to you."

He said, "No, Mother. To this day, no one has ever approached me."

After that we just talked about it. It was a rough period. I said to Paul the next day, "I told you I knew something terrible was wrong. It's not a whore. He's a homosexual. Oh my God, Paul, what will we do?"

Paul: *We discussed things and decided we'd better take him to a psychiatrist. We thought surely a psychiatrist could straighten him out. We didn't think he had to be gay. We thought he was confused. Well, we found out he wasn't.*

■

One day at work I saw a letter from Marsha on my desk. I got this funny feeling in the pit of my stomach. I knew it was going to be something bad; so I quickly went to the ladies' lounge to open the letter.

Instead, it was just a nice long letter saying she'd like to talk to me alone, and would I come get her at the college where she was a student. I drove up to get her. When we started home, Marsha asked to drive. I thought, "My goodness! She never wants to do that."

We hadn't gone far when she started talking. She said, "I know you're wondering why I wanted to talk to you alone. I don't know whether you've suspected it or not, but I'm gay."

I said, "Well, yes, I have suspected it." I continued talking to keep from crying and sobbing and screaming. I didn't cry in front of her. I'll put it that way.

We had a nice, long talk all the way home. She asked me if she should tell her dad that weekend. I felt that we ought to wait a little while and let me adjust first, because I figured we'd have to pick her dad up off the floor or the ceiling or somewhere and take him to the hospital.

For a few days, this mother handled her feelings alone. She felt that she had to protect her husband. Her unshared grief finally boiled over, and she told her husband during a family argument.

I didn't find out from Marsha. I found out from my wife. Marsha had talked with her earlier. Ruth and I were having a family spat when she said something to the effect that on top of all the other problems we had, we also had to deal with the fact that we had a daughter who was homosexual. Everything stopped right there.

I was bewildered. I was hurt by the fact that my daughter didn't trust me enough to tell me. I was very disappointed and began wondering just how shallow our relationship had been. Where had I failed? Why was she afraid of me? Where had I gone wrong in raising her so that she didn't feel secure in talking to me? My first resolve was not so much to talk to her about being gay, but to talk about our relationship.

I thought about it awhile and decided I had to have open communication with Marsha. I wrote her a letter and told her that I didn't understand all of it; that I had questions I wanted to discuss privately. I felt pleased that I had established a line of communication with her.

∎

Don came out to me after another son let it slip that he was gay. I have four sons and a daughter. My other boys had been talking about Don and his "queer" friends. When I objected to the way they were talking, one said, "Well, Mom, you know Don's gay."

I said, "Don't say that about him. After all, he's your brother." I became very defensive and talked about it being okay that Don was not an athlete. I started to cry. I said, "I don't know why I'm crying. I don't believe this. I don't think it's true." A little while later, the phone rang.

One of my other sons had called Don and told him, "You'd better call Mother. We just told her you're gay. She's all upset."

My first question when Don called was, "Don, are you gay?" And he said, "Yes, but you've always known that." I said, "When did you find out?" He answered, "When I was about three or four."

I felt that I had failed. I thought, "How am I going to deal with this? What will the neighbors say?" I had a lot of bad information stored in the back of my head.

It's a blow to your ego to think you're such a competent and perceptive parent and then find you have a gay child. You think you know your child so well and then find out he knew this at a young age and didn't tell. You feel you really missed the boat on some things.

Sometimes parents sense what their child is about to tell them. Inadvertently, they give their child a double message, "Tell me, but don't tell me." Most of us want to hold back the news.

Sarah tried to tell us over the phone. She began to cry. I told her I knew something was seriously wrong. I had had thoughts that she might be lesbian, but I kept pushing them out of my mind. I told her to call back whenever she thought she could talk.

I didn't really want to hear it. I probably could have helped by saying, "Sarah, are you trying to tell us you're gay?" But I was afraid she'd say yes. And I wasn't about to take a chance on that.

It was about three days later when we got the letter, and I didn't even want to open it. It was a loving letter, a caring letter. She told us she had been aware of her gayness since she was twelve. She wasn't ashamed of it. She had found somebody she loved who loved her. For the first time in her life she wasn't lonely anymore.

Herb and I cried when we read the letter because it was full of pain. It's a letter no parent wants to receive. Then we thought, "Where do we go from here?"

THE PARADOX: PAIN AND SORROW
VERSUS FREEDOM AND FULFILLMENT

All of us, by the time we have reached the middle years, have had a full share of disillusionment and disappointment. We have learned that the enchanting folk tales of our childhood have no literal truth. Cinderella has a fifty-percent chance of ending in the divorce courts, frogs don't change into princes, and ugly ducklings usually grow up to be ugly ducks. If we are lucky, we learn to accept reality, roll with the punches, and become philosophical about our disappointments.

Yet there is a special poignancy where shattered expectations about our children are concerned. One compensation for life's bruises is that our children will "do us honor." We have given them love and made sacrifices for them. In return, consciously or unconsciously, we expect our children to make up for the past, en-

rich the present, and represent the future. We think they will accomplish great things, bring us the joy of happy marriages, and
give us grandchildren.

Few experiences cause us to realize the folly of these unrealistic expectations as quickly or as effectively as learning that one of
our children is gay. Our grief is intense, and we have trouble giving it a name because it touches every phase of our lives. Often, it
is likened to having a death in the family. And there *is* a death—
of the familiar beliefs and hopes that have kept us going through
our child-raising years.

Unaware of any alternatives, we grieve as our self-worth is threatened. We think, "My child is sick, I am sick, our family life is sick.
I hurt my baby." A feeling of horror comes over us as we often
admit to ourselves, "I do not approve of what my child is. He or
she is strange, weird, perverted. I'm not sure I want to be around
people like that." Remorse and tears can become our daily com-
panions as we are caught by the opinions that fill the libraries and
the airwaves. No one really knows, yet everyone thinks he or she
knows. Even so-called experts tell us opposite ideas about cause,
"cure," lifestyle, and even what homosexuality is. We experience
an emotional loss.

*I thought, "Oh my God. My daughter is a pervert!" I felt that I was the
world's biggest failure. Every father I saw was better than I was.*

■

*Every book that I had seen said homosexuality was caused by a distur-
bance in the family. They said that there was usually an absent or rejecting father and a domineering, seductive, or binding kind of mother. I
thought about how much Jack worked when the kids were small and the
fact that I was the one who stayed home and took care of them. I twisted it
all around and said, "Yes, maybe we are like that. Maybe there was something really wrong with us."*

We grieve in our churches as we listen to the religious attacks
against our children. We wonder if our child is living sinfully, and
we fear for his or her salvation. We hear our religious leaders

speak out against homosexuality and find ourselves in distress as unthinking church members voice unkind thoughts. We experience a spiritual loss.

Right after we found out about our lesbian daughter, our church began exploring the idea of openly accepting gays and lesbians. I found it hard to sit near people who were saying, "We shouldn't have to vote on that." Some of the members even passed around a petition to keep lesbians and gays out of the church. That was hard to handle. I'd come home from church and scream and yell that if those were the kind of people God wanted in his church, then God didn't need me.

We grieve over the loss of grandchildren. Many of us know this feeling is self-centered, but that does not lessen it. This desire is so basic that few parents escape the yearning. It is almost universal. It does not matter that some of us will have grandchildren from our other children. We want them from each of our children. We assume our name, our genes, will not be carried on by our gay child. We do not, as yet, know that many gay people do have children. The loss we feel could be called a biological loss.

I've always loved babies and kids. One of my first thoughts was that Mary will never bring home a nice young man and say, "This is it, Mom. This is the man I love." I'll never have grandkids from Mary. She'll never have a child that I can think of as her child.

■

I've had dreams of a successful family with my three children going out and getting married and having their own children. I'd have all these grandchildren to play with. All at once, one-third of my trio goes off on a tangent.

We grieve over our loss of status as we are faced with unfamiliar shame. We have an uneasy feeling, as we become aware that we are associated with an "undesirable" group. We fear that anger and rejection will be directed toward us when people learn we have a gay or lesbian child. We are confused about how to treat our child's partner, and we do not know how our child will fit into our everyday life. We are worried about the effect on our other children and grandchildren, our parents and siblings, our friends, our neighbors, the people we work with. This is a social loss.

My husband doesn't want his family to know. To me that means he's ashamed of Mary. But I myself hesitate. I'd like to tell my good friend. We grew up together, and I would like for her to know. But I don't know what she would think of me or Mary. She makes a lot of negative comments about gays.

And we usually experience our multiple losses alone. We have to go about our lives with a secret pain that we cannot share. We cannot often hear consoling words from our friends. It is understandable that parents often describe their reactions in such highly charged terms as failure, fright, disappointment, shame, and guilt. Occasionally, parents will say that it would be easier to handle the death of a child than having a gay child. While this reaction does not usually last, it is a painful example of how damaging homophobia is in our society. The reason for such intense feelings may be that the normal death of a child carries no shame, while having a gay child is seen as bringing lifelong dishonor to the family.

Sooner or later, however, parents have to go beyond the cultural messages of rejection and hatred if they are to feel any peace. Facing the problem may cost us a great deal of time and pain. It is frightening to let go of established guideposts when there are only shaky and unproven ones to replace them. And there may be little help from any of the traditional sources such as church, social groups, extended family, or even close friends. Parents must sink or swim by their own efforts.

But swim many of them do. The decision to go against hurtful societal views often does more than just help them survive. The act of confronting homosexuality openly and courageously can become a source of freedom and fulfillment in the family. It can strengthen affection between the parents and the child. It can begin a movement toward restoring the wholeness of everyone involved.

We know that some parents may choose to remain caught in despondency. This exacts its own high cost. These parents take on the prejudices of the culture and do damage to themselves. By refusing to get involved in the struggle to change their inaccurate perceptions, they never stop struggling.

But a move to a positive view is not easy. The glimmer of the "up" feelings is often countered by the "down" messages regularly heard in day-to-day interactions. Parents have often referred to this experience as similar to being on a roller coaster, with its sudden, unpredictable ups and downs.

With time and effort, though, the balance can be tipped toward a positive experience. More independent thinking and a sense of personal power are often reported.

INITIAL PARENTAL ACTIONS

Before exploring features of the road to a positive resolution, it is useful to identify some of the ways that parents react immediately after finding out. There are four actions that parents may take that are typical. The first three lead to parental despair; the fourth opens possibilities for change and, eventually, inner peace. They are: breaking contact, trying to change the child, ignoring the issue, and accepting reality.

Breaking Contact

There are some parents who choose to cast out the gay child completely. We have met many such children. They look at us with longing and puzzlement, wondering why it is that we can accept them and their parents cannot.

When I was thirteen, there was a boy in junior high with me whom I liked a lot. In fact, I was in love with him. My sexual feeling for him scared me, but still that was how I felt. He was in an automobile accident, and for a while I thought he might die. I often cried because he meant so much to me. There was nothing sexual between us.

My mother noticed how unhappy I was and kept asking what was wrong. We had always been close so I finally got up the nerve to tell her that I was gay. She got upset and threw me out. She said she wasn't going to let me hurt my younger brother and sisters.

I didn't know what to do. I got some of my clothes and left. My dad was coming up the walk as I was leaving. He wasn't too upset. He just said, "You know how your mother is," and went inside.

I went to a massage parlor I had heard of and asked for a job. They were nice to me and even let me sleep there. I got the job, and I have been working there for five years now. I don't know what I would have done if they hadn't helped me out. I don't go to school anymore, but I'm making loads of money. I have more money than any kid my age that I know.

But I miss my family. Sometimes I walk up and down the street hoping my mom will let me in. Once she came out and told me that when the kids get bigger, I could visit, but so far I haven't been able to go in. Sometimes I go near where my dad works and see him when he goes out to lunch. He shakes my hand and says, "How's it going?" But he doesn't ask me to come home either. Someday maybe my parents will take me back. I keep hoping.

David is lucky. He still lives. He still has hope. Experts tell us that many "throw-away" children die tragically, alone, with no one to care. There is an unknown toll of rejected gay children who become victims of the seamy side of street life—drug addiction, prostitution, crime, and disease.

Parents who cut off their relationship with their child pay a heavy price. They can push their son or daughter out of their lives, but not out of their hearts. They have to expend a great deal of energy maintaining a façade as they go about their daily routine. Weighed down with guilt, anger, and disappointment, they are confined to a life without their children.

Punishing the victim never solves the problem—and our gay and lesbian children have become the victims of a vast array of false information and prejudicial treatment.

Trying to Change the Child

A large number of parents focus their energies on strategies to change their children. Recent research holds that fundamental sexual orientation does not change. Still, there are three ways in which parents pursue false hopes: taking the child to a psychotherapist, leading the child to religious conversion, and/or encouraging the child to have a sexual relationship with a person of the opposite sex.

Taking the Child to a Psychotherapist. Psychotherapy as a source for the change of a person's sexual orientation is often one of the first ideas a parent considers. Thinking of a child's homosexual orientation as an illness draws parents toward the idea of a medical cure.

One couple decided to take their son to a psychiatrist when they first learned that he was gay. The psychiatrist said he could cure their son if their bank account were large enough, and asked to see their bank statement. He told them they would have to spend several thousand dollars. This unethical behavior created guilt for the parents, as they were not wealthy enough to afford his services. Fortunately, this couple learned that the psychiatrist could not support his claim, and they did not fall victim to the sham. The most that health-care professionals can do is help families learn to accept the homosexual member in a constructive way. A growing number of knowledgeable, responsible therapists are committed to supporting such a goal.

Leading the Child to Religious Conversion. Some parents look to their religion as a way of getting their children into a heterosexual lifestyle. Our gay and lesbian children, however, have for years attended houses of worship hearing of the love of God for all except themselves. They have come to an awareness of their homosexuality slowly and usually painfully, never casually. Many report feeling desolation and bewilderment as they became aware of being attracted to members of their own sex. Often they prayed and hoped for a change from God. At times they considered suicide as the only way out. Some wanted to be what they were hearing in the churches they should be, and yet they knew they could not be. Others denied who they were for years, even decades.

Often, religious leaders themselves are poorly informed about the biological and social aspects of homosexuality. Frequently they do not acknowledge that there are widely differing positions among religious leaders. They may not even be accurate about biblical perspective and interpretation. Families can be ripped apart when they encounter such insensitivity and ignorance.

Religion may offer support and understanding, but it cannot alter sexual orientation.

Encouraging the Child to Have a Relationship with a Person of the Opposite Sex. Heterosexual expression is a familiar part of life. Many parents have been taught that this is the only natural way. They often hope and believe that a good sexual experience with someone of the opposite sex will turn their gay son or lesbian daughter around. The message to the gay person is "Just give it a chance. You'll see how great my kind of love is, and everything will be just fine." What this often does is create heartache for both the gay person and for the partner who is being used in an experiment doomed to failure.

Parents who cling to the illusion that change can occur, whether in the name of Freud, God, or opposite-sex love, put themselves and their child through unnecessary anguish. It is an exercise in futility.

The next story tells about one young man who tried all the above ideas in order to change. He is still gay, but he and others are suffering from guilt and confusion. No one has any suggestions for him or for his family now. He has tried them all.

John is filled with guilt, depression, and self-loathing. From early adolescence he has realized that he is gay. He has struggled against his nature—praying a lot and suffering in isolation. His father, now retired, was a minister who considered homosexuality to be a sinful choice.

Hoping a heterosexual relationship would change him, John married a young woman who was his friend. She was kind and understanding, went to his church, and was totally dedicated to him. They lived together for a year. It was a year of agony for him. Finally, he left her and secretly moved in with a man.

Buffeted by the punishing statements he heard, John found no peace in his homosexual lifestyle. In the hopes that he could feel sexually attracted to women, he went to a Christian psychologist and joined a religious group dedicated to changing gay men. Neither effort worked.

In desperation he confessed his secret life to his brother who thought it was his duty to inform the rest of the family. John's father took him to their present minister, and in an emotional session John confessed his "sin" and asked for forgiveness. He moved back in with his wife.

A year later the couple had a child who died from sudden infant death syndrome. John thinks God is punishing him for being gay. Most of the people in his church agree with him. John's wife is suffering a hell of her own. She cannot feel secure and wonders how long he will stay with her this time.

This couple is in misery because the husband is being forced to accept a lifestyle into which he simply cannot fit. Their hopes for happiness are tied up in the idea that somehow John's sexual nature will change.

Our gay children are brave, strong, and searching. They are what they are. They will remain what they are. Acceptance by parents gives them a boost in coping with a tough world. Trying to change them adds enormously to their burden.

Ignoring the Issue: The Ostrich Effect

Another response that tempts parents is a decision to ignore the situation, yet still maintain contact. We also call this the ostrich effect. Small children, when fearful of thunderstorms, try to feel safe by crawling under the blankets and pulling the covers over their heads. "If we can't see it or hear it, maybe it will go away." Adults sometimes handle problems this same way. The child within needs to feel safe from fear, and the denial of the situation can be helpful for a while. It gives some people time to absorb the information.

Some parents do not give up that denial system, and continue to say, "You've told me you're gay. I hope you know what you're doing. Don't talk about it with me anymore. I don't want to know about that part of your life. We'll keep everything else in our interactions like it was before."

The internal and external conflicts that absorb mothers and fathers in their early grief do not spontaneously disappear. These conflicts, left unchallenged, keep such parents precariously balanced. They cannot break off with their child. Nor can they examine and revise their ideas that created the conflict. So they silently stay on this uncommitted course. In essence, they try to move back to a safer, earlier time when for them the problem of society's homophobia did not exist.

Children who experience this response sense the double bind the parents are feeling. Often they are caught in the same bind. Many want to sit down with their parents and teach them all they have learned. They want to share their joys and hurts, but they know they cannot bring up the subject. Issues surrounding homosexuality form a barrier that separates children from parents.

Mike is a case in point. He loves his parents, and they love him. Being a teenager was hell for him as he became aware that he was gay. He took the extreme step of attempting suicide. Shaken by the experience, he began to turn himself around. Like so many lesbians and gays, he finally came to say, "I am a homosexual, a queer, a faggot. I've always heard it is bad to be one of 'them,' but I know that I'm okay. No one will convince me that I am not."

Mike now has a bedrock feeling of self-worth, which led to the decision to tell his parents. The telling itself was calm and uneventful. But there was firm resistance to any follow-up. His sense of well-being gave him the courage to be a leader in the fight for gay rights. He tried often to share his activities with his parents, but they weren't interested. Mike attended family gatherings, but his lifestyle was never mentioned. He listened to all the personal stories of his brothers, sisters, and cousins, but knew he could never speak of his own. He was excluded from equal participation in family life and was relegated to being a passive observer.

When Mike became an effective activist for gay rights, he was invited to appear on television. One night, Mike dropped by his family home for a visit. His father came into the living room with a gun, pointed it at him, and said, "If I see you on television, I will kill you." Mike left, shaken and fearful. He did appear on TV.

A year has passed and the family has drifted back into the old rou-tine. Mike visits, listens, doesn't speak about his own life, and wonders if his father could really hurt him. He feels that he is sitting on a volcano, but he says the greater tragedy for him is the determined silence with which his parents treat his life outside the family. Despite the fact that his fam-ily did not come through for him, he has continued his work for gay rights.

While the threat to Mike's life is extreme, less dramatic forms of the ostrich effect are very common and take their toll. Pushing away a part of life that is important never solves any problems. The problems haunt us when we are frightened and weak, and we find ourselves taking actions that later fill us with remorse. Our emo-tional responses can be held back only so long. For everyone con-cerned it is important that the ideas we have about homosexuality be carefully studied.

Accepting Reality

Fortunately, there is another response that any parent can choose to take—accepting reality. Such acceptance is a process that is often slow and uncomfortable. But for those who stay with it, the rewards are great. The people we interviewed are examples of those who chose this path.

On the surface, these parents appear to have little in common. Some are conservative, others liberal. Some are divorced or wid-owed, others have the traditional, two-parent family structure. Re-ligious beliefs fall into a wide range, from being deeply and traditionally religious to being agnostic or atheist. Almost all felt negative about or aloof from gayness before they knew of their children's homosexuality.

There is a common thread shared by all. Our interviewed par-ents gave top priority to maintaining a good relationship with their children. As one father put it, "When I found out, I soon de-cided I had to either stand with my son or support the rejecting attitudes of the society. I chose to stand with my child."

Such parents often reported that they had a moment when they realized that this child of theirs, labeled a "social reject," is the same child they held in their arms as an infant. It is the child they nurtured through good times and bad, and who gave them love and trust. The basic decision they made then was to let nothing interfere with the caring relationship.

I told myself I didn't care how Dave, my husband, reacted. I didn't care what he did. There was nothing that would make me kick Carol out of the house. Never would I tell her she couldn't come to see us. There were many things that went through my mind. I wondered how I could know Carol's friends, how I could still be a part of her life.

■

Right after Steve told us, things were really bad. I remember one time when he wanted to go out and I wouldn't give him the car; but he was determined to go and meet this guy anyway. He dressed and left. I got in the car and was going to the store when I saw him walking down Main Street. I just felt terrible for him. Even though I was upset, I was feeling sorry for him too. I made a rule for myself that I wasn't going to browbeat him anymore or get him to conform to my rules. I wasn't going to do anything to hurt him again.

■

When I found out Don was gay, it was hard, certainly. But a day or two after I knew, I was sitting by myself and thought, "He's still the same son who asked me for five dollars this morning; he's the same boy who was here for breakfast, who took out the trash, who wrecked the car. His sexuality doesn't have anything to do with his integrity or his ability to love or his worth."

I guess I could have said, "Get out of my life and don't ever come back." And he could have agreed. But he wouldn't have been out of my life. I would have been the one to lose. I would have lost the things we have shared and all our closeness. He's a loving, honest, and wonderful son. He told me he was gay, and he's still a loving, honest, and wonderful son. I don't think you have to be anything but full of love to learn to accept your child.

These parents also realized a fundamental truth—their gay and lesbian children cannot change. The prime area for change would have to be in the parents' own attitudes and ideas. This started our parents on a challenging course. It required that they "unlearn" the myths of the culture and stand against them. It was scary but freeing. Love for their children told them they were on the right path.

The rest of this book details the process that parents go through to accept their children and change their own attitudes. As part of this process, parents have to modify their internal belief system, learn the facts, confront the prevailing cultural view, and move to new levels of understanding. This often arduous course produces personal and familial changes of extraordinary value. These parents, with both gay and nongay children, develop an inner strength that allows all of them to confront life's challenges realistically.

NOTE FOR CHAPTER ONE

1. Adele Starr, statement in *About Our Children,* a pamphlet formerly published by P-FLAG. For directions on how to obtain a list of current P-FLAG publications and a Recommended Reading List, see Bibliography.

■ TWO ■

WHAT WE
LEARNED
FROM BOOKS

*T*he negative feelings I had about homosexuality came from everything I had contact with as I was growing up: from my mother, from the kids in school, from outhouse and toilet walls, from books and magazines.

■

In my own growing up, I'm not sure how I managed to pick up only misinformation about gays. Yet how could it have been otherwise, as our society is rampantly homophobic? Until recent years, misinformation was the only game in town.

Parents today are in a situation somewhat analogous to the children of my generation. I grew up in the 1920s and 1930s. Sexual matters, even the simplest facts, like where babies came from, were regarded as dangerous. There was a conspiracy of silence.

These same children, now grown up and parents, have once again been victimized by a conspiracy of silence and have had to rely on gossip instead of guidance—this time concerning homosexuality.

■

Neither my husband nor I knew anything about homosexuality outside of the gutter language that we had heard. You know, queers and fags and words like that. We simply didn't have enough information to have done any independent thinking on the subject. But how many of us do have information on homosexuality until it confronts us?

Armed only with myths, we, as parents of gay children, were poorly prepared to defend ourselves against the shock and confusion we felt at first. We had been victimized on several counts. We were hurt by the outdated, unsubstantiated and often opposing "expert" opinions that floated around in the scientific community. We were hurt by the whispers, smirks, innuendos, and jokes that were an acceptable part of our social community. We were hurt by the bigotry that is present in so many of our religious communities.

Yet, our children, as we knew them, did not fit the image of the ugly myths we had grown up with. Our daughters and sons were not weird people. They didn't look peculiar. They weren't molesting children. They weren't harming society in any way. They were solid citizens who were making valuable contributions to society with dignity and courage.

We have heard a story about people who spent their lives chained in a dark cave. The prisoners saw the reality of the outside world through shadows on the cave wall. Their concept of the world was a gross distortion, but it was the only truth they had. When we found out that our children were gay, we were like those prisoners in the cave. Our homophobia created our prison, and our beliefs, the old myths, were like the shadows on the wall. They were all we had to make some kind of sense of our situation. Replacing these myths with proven facts helped set us free. The facts gave us a base from which we could move into the light of reality.

It wasn't easy to unlearn old myths. We were confused, scared, and feeling guilty that we had failed as parents. Perhaps somebody knew something that we didn't know. Perhaps we had misjudged our children and were seeing them only through rose-colored glasses.

Floundering, many of us did what we had done frequently in the past. We tried to get a handle on things by looking for the origin, the cause. We asked ourselves, "What causes it? Did we cause it? Did somebody entice them into it and lead them astray?"

People who are further along in their acceptance tell us that we should not be concerned with cause; that we should be concerned with believing that being gay or lesbian is okay. And that it is a step many of us would eventually come to. But in the beginning, the cause of homosexuality filled our minds and could not be ignored.

There was another, more subtle reason that led us toward the search for cause. We hoped that a natural explanation for homosexuality could be found. We wanted to discover that gayness is a normal part of life, and therefore justifiable. What is natural is acceptable, whether we like it or not. Armed with such knowledge, we would have something that could calm our damaging inner voices and lessen our confusion and guilt. Not having knowledge left us at the mercy of opinions.

Some lesbians and gays understandably resent it when parents are concerned about cause—especially if they don't understand that grieving parents first need to get out from under blame. The patience of gay children toward their parents' concern about cause is often rewarded. Parental anxiety about cause brings the first real confrontation with the shadows of old myths and usually acts as a spur to learning more about homosexuality.

After I'd go to bed at night, I'd mull things over in my mind. "Have I really been that dominant a mother? Curt made many of the decisions. He had his thumb on everything. We also made many decisions together, and even though I am more outspoken, that doesn't mean I'm dominant. I know

Curt didn't play ball with the boys, but he was always around and available for the other youngsters and was interested in everything they did." I didn't see why this was happening to us, because we had done a lot "right." At least to us it felt right.

■

I worried a lot about why. Society has always said if your child does not measure up to the norm, it is the mother's fault. I am divorced, and I kept wondering if that had anything to do with Jay's being gay. For a while, I even thought that one of "those" guys had done something to my son to entice him into a terrible life.

■

I was always much closer to Brian than my husband was. Brian and I often used to sit around and talk. I thought, "Was that unhealthy?" I looked back at all of our family life to see what was wrong in it. I figured there had to be something bad to cause this. At that time the only information I had was that homosexuality was caused by some sort of problem in the family.

■

The first thing you want to know is "Did I cause it?" We're taught that it's shameful and perverted to be gay, and when it happens to you, in your family, the guilt comes out immediately. So the first thing you're interested in is how much of it is your fault. I worried that I had hurt my daughter.

Between the late 1940s and the early 1980s, the most comprehensive studies about homosexuality were done by researchers at the Alfred C. Kinsey Institute for Sex Research at the University of Indiana at Bloomington: *Sexual Behavior in the Human Male* (1948) and *Sexual Behavior in the Human Female* (1952); and the more recent book by Bell, Weinberg, and Hammersmith, entitled *Sexual Preference: Its Development in Men and Women* (1982). They were the pioneering works on human sexuality, and we made extensive use of them in the first edition.

As continuing researchers always build on the shoulders of those giants who went before them, some very recent research has opened exciting new ways of understanding the homosexual/heterosexual dichotomy. The puzzle pieces are not all in place by any means, but as parents we are grateful for the understanding and freedom that this research brings to our cause. We will describe these new studies later in this chapter.

We will examine twelve of the most commonly held myths, beginning with the ones that are the most difficult for parents—the myths concerning cause. Though there are numerous myths about cause, we chose four of the most common to report on. The "cause myths" (#1–#4) are followed by a personal statement about cause that is based on our research and experience.

MYTH #1—NEUROTIC FAMILY PATTERNS CAUSE HOMOSEXUALITY

Most parents have suffered in one way or another from being told that a gay child is produced by a neurotic family. Such a family is described as being the combination of a dominant or seductive mother and a weak or distant father. There is a scientific ring to this falsehood that makes it difficult to ignore. We decided to find out the source of this myth.

Until the gay rights movement began in 1969, there was little research on homosexuality. The few studies that did exist tended to support the biases of the culture.

One work that was widely quoted was published in a book by Irving Bieber et al., *Homosexuality: A Psychoanalytic Study*.[1] It stated that male homosexuality is caused by an engulfing mother and/or a weak, distant, or hostile father.

Critics have pointed out that this study was characterized by the following poor research methods: only people who were in psychoanalysis were studied, no attempt was made to have a representative sample, there was no comparative control group, and the researchers made no attempt to eliminate researcher bias. As a result, the opinions presented in the study were just that—opinions, with no basis of fact to back them up. The study revealed more about psychoanalytic patients than about gays.[2]

Fortunately, the Alfred C. Kinsey Institute for Sex Research also decided to study the question of why some people are homosexual. The results of this work were published in the book *Sexual Preference* by Bell, Weinberg, and Hammersmith.[3]

These authors used careful methods in order to ensure that their conclusions would not be colored by old myths. Researchers Bell, Weinberg, and Hammersmith questioned 979 homosexuals and 477 heterosexuals who made up a representative and matched sample of the total population.[4] Their meticulous study took ten years to complete—three years in which to collect the data, five years to analyze it, and another two years to check it.[5] They found that family backgrounds had little or no effect on a person's eventual sexual orientation. One of the central passages in the book sums up a major finding that can help parents drop their guilt about cause.

> For the benefit of readers who are concerned about what parents may do to influence their children's sexual preference, we would restate our findings another way. No particular phenomenon of family life can be singled out, on the basis of our findings, as especially consequential for either homosexual or heterosexual development. You may supply your sons with footballs and your daughters with dolls, but no one can guarantee that they will enjoy them. *What we seem to have identified . . . is a pattern of feelings and reactions within the child that cannot be traced back to a single social or psychological root;* indeed, homosexuality may arise from a biological precursor (as do left-handedness and allergies, for example) that parents cannot control. In short, to concerned parents, we cannot recommend anything beyond the care, sympathy, and devotion that good parents presumably lavish on all their children anyway.[6]

The accurate studies tell us there are neurotic family patterns and there are loving family patterns. Both types of families produce heterosexual and homosexual children.[7]

MYTH #2—ACTING LIKE A SISSY OR TOMBOY CAUSES PEOPLE TO BE GAY

Some gay and lesbian children were at odds with their parents when they were growing up. A number of our parents reported that they were often left feeling frustrated and confused as they realized their child didn't follow the typical interest patterns of children their age; for example, a son who didn't enjoy competitive sports, such as baseball, or a daughter who did. Going outside of what our society considers typical—expected masculine or feminine behavior—is called by Bell, Weinberg, and Hammersmith "gender nonconformity."[8] It often left parents feeling like failures as they wondered, "Why isn't he or she like the other boys or girls? Did I fail to provide a good role model?" The following excerpts show the problem:

Matt, my gay son, didn't fit the mold, the macho male mold, that his brother, John, did. Matt didn't have any interest in sports. His interests were along a different line. He tried baseball, but it was hard for him because he was a little bit on the stout side. He was the last one to be put into the game, and he was the strike-out king. Oh, I was in Boy Scouts with him, but as he got older, it seemed we communicated less and less. There was a big wall between us.

One time when Matt was in high school, I sat him down and told him that I felt this wall; that I wanted to break it down but that it had to be a two-way street. I asked him to help me. He said he would, but we were never successful. And that wall was there until he told us he was gay.

■

I suffered a great deal of guilt about the way I had related to Alex when he was growing up. When he was a baby, things were fine, but as soon as he got to where he could go outside and play, I failed him miserably. I feel I didn't do enough with him. I tried to play with him as I did with Joe and Vickie, but he wouldn't go by the rules. He always tried to change them. He just wouldn't conform. I took him to things like Hi-Y and Cub Scouts and participated with him, but when it came to relating to each other every day, we just couldn't seem to hit it off.

By the time he was ten or twelve, he was very frustrated and dissatisfied. I think it was worse when he got old enough for competition. He could compete, but he didn't feel that he could. Sometime in there I think he put a name to his difference. He was very bright, and he read a lot.

I was frustrated because I didn't know what was wrong. I remember one time I told him I felt cheated because I never had the relationship with him that I wanted. I said, "You never let me do anything with you," which he didn't. He didn't fit the mold, my mold. I was probably terrified to bend enough to fit his mold, which is really terrible to say.

These fathers and their sons suffered from their inability to understand each other. Neither side had the necessary information to help break down the wall, even though they wanted to. Mothers, too, recalled being concerned about the "gender nonconformity" of their sons. Many of our interviewed parents had trouble admitting that their sons acted in any way feminine.

From a very early age I could see that Mike was what you might call more feminine than the masculine "ideal." We had to decide as parents how we were going to deal with that. He enjoyed a lot of things that girls typically like. It wasn't extreme, but he liked music, art, quiet games, and that sort of thing. He didn't go for rough play or for athletics in general.

I decided that I didn't want to make Mike self-conscious about his nature, but at the same time I did want to make "masculine" things available to him. So we went out of our way to teach him how to play ball. We did a lot of sports together as a family, which was fun because we all liked them. We went camping and did other rough outdoor activities. And from time to time we tried to interest him in things like Boy Scouts and Little League.

We would encourage him to take part in the usual "boy" activities, but we didn't want to make him feel uncomfortable if he didn't choose them. And he usually didn't choose them. He didn't like the rough-and-tumble. Although he did like camping and had some interest in certain sports, he didn't like contact sports. So we decided to keep off his back and let him do what appealed to him. Our goal was to make him comfortable with being whatever he was and not restrict him.

The nonconformity of a son tends to create more conflict than does such behavior in a daughter. Still, many parents reported that they noticed their daughter's lack of interest in traditionally "feminine" activities.

Thinking back over the years I remember there were several times when the possibility that Mary might be gay crossed my mind. But each time I brushed it from my mind and even felt guilty about having the thought.

Once when Mary was three years old she asked, "Do I always have to be a girl?" When she was growing up, she liked the companionship of boys her age. She always enjoyed athletics even though she was not that good. She was never very interested in dolls. I can still picture her as a little girl with a softball in one hand, a bat in the other, and a toy gun in the holster on her hip.

■

When Melinda was little she was very much a tomboy, as I had been. I thought, "Well, she's a tomboy, but that's fine." She never did play with dolls. Neither did I. I had one doll in my whole life, and I hated it. I believed she was just behaving like I did.

I wondered if Melinda was gay when she was in high school, because her best friend was a tough-looking girl, and I didn't like that. I even asked Melinda if her friend was gay, but I never did ask Melinda if she was.

Even though we have many examples of parents who noticed nonconformity in their child, we also have examples from those who did not.

Jerry dated a little in high school. As I think back over it, there wasn't too much about his relationship with girls that would have led me to believe he was gay. He was a very good dancer, had a good personality, and, if I say so myself, was very good-looking. Girls were always around here clamoring over him.

■

I was never so surprised in my life as when Cathy told me she was a lesbian. She was just what you would expect a little girl to be. She played with dolls and had crushes on boys. She even dated a lot in high school. She chose to wear dresses and was very feminine.

■

My son was "all boy" the whole time he was growing up. He liked sports and fishing. He was a good pitcher in Little League.

Usually, parents felt there was some lack in themselves that created the feminine actions of their sons or the masculine actions of their daughters, although parents were not as concerned about this kind of behavior on the part of the girls. They believed that such actions by boys indicated an unhappy and maladjusted child. They were also afraid that their sons would be subject to ridicule from classmates. As a result, some parents pressured their young children to change their natural behavior.

The authors of *Sexual Preference* believe that gender nonconformity may signal homosexuality for many gays and lesbians. But it is not a cause. Of course, it would have been better if we parents had known that we had little to do with the gender nonconformity of our children. Unfortunately for everyone concerned, we did not.

We hope that this information will clear away some of the guilt that parents and children often feel when they look back over some of the parent-child conflicts of the early years together. As one father said so well, "Now I see that the problem in our relationship wasn't my fault, and it wasn't his. We were just caught up in something we couldn't understand."

MYTH #3—HOMOSEXUAL SEDUCTION CAUSES CHILDREN TO BE GAY

No other lie causes as much damage to our gay and lesbian children as does this one. People mount political hate campaigns in the name of saving the children. These campaigns have led to the denial of basic democratic rights for gay and lesbian persons. Teachers lose their jobs if they are gay, even though there is absolutely no evidence that their being openly gay or otherwise will have any impact on their students' sexuality.

As with many of the ideas about cause, the authors of *Sexual Preference* found that neither gays nor lesbians were seduced into the homosexual lifestyle.[9] There was a significant period of time between becoming aware of being gay or lesbian and acting on that awareness.[10] In fact, lesbian and gay adolescents often think they are alone. It is a frightening and sad time for them and can sometimes lead to tragic consequences.

MYTH #4—A TRAUMATIC EVENT WITH A PERSON OF THE OPPOSITE SEX CAN CAUSE HOMOSEXUALITY

There was no evidence to support this idea in the study done by Bell, Weinberg, and Hammersmith. Traumatic events caused pain for both gay and nongay people, but did not cause them to change their sexual orientation.[11] Being gay or lesbian does not mean being angry with people of the opposite sex. It simply means being sexually attracted to people of the same sex.

A PERSONAL NOTE FROM THE AUTHORS ABOUT CAUSE

Each time a new research theory comes out about cause, parents tend to look inside themselves, as well as at their total family life. They often say to themselves, "Did I do that? Was our family like that? Maybe someone has found out something that will indict me! Maybe I am guilty of a crime against my son or daughter!" After a while—when they are able to discriminate between fact and opinion—parents learn to reject the damage caused by their own negative thoughts and by the false opinions of others.

As of this writing the definitive cause of homosexuality is not known. What we can say is that recent research in general has discredited the idea that parents are the cause, and those guilt feelings should be completely discarded.

Before we go on with other myths that are not concerned with cause, we should explain our bias about this question. We lean toward a biological cause for two reasons. First, the latest and best research points that way. Second, it fits our experience.

We also want to see an end to the blame game that raises its ugly head with alarming regularity. When energy is spent on establishing blame, little is done to resolve issues. But, more than this, we believe that our society will accept gayness only if the vast majority of its citizens see it as a naturally occurring event. If most people understood that a certain percentage of society will be gay no matter what their family background is, or what their sexual experiences were, then gay people would have a better chance of living their lives free from fears of retaliation. There would be no need for books like this one. Parents could accept their children's gay orientation as easily as they now accept left-handedness (which used to be considered wrong or even a sign of bewitchment).

MYTH #5—GAY AND LESBIAN PEOPLE ARE MENTALLY SICK

In the face of overwhelming odds and much adversity, the majority of gays and lesbians are psychologically healthy. They are remarkably similar to their heterosexual counterparts. A minority of both groups are disturbed; a majority of both groups show good mental health. The percentages are the same.[12]

In a landmark study in 1957, Evelyn Hooker found that there was no significant difference in the mental health of homosexuals and heterosexuals.[13] This finding was confirmed by other studies. As a result, both the American Psychological Association and the American Psychiatric Association no longer list homosexuality as a mental illness.

Another study compared lesbian women to heterosexual women. Mark Freedman reported his work in the article,"Stimulus-

Response: Homosexuals May Be Healthier Than Straights."[14] He found that lesbian women often functioned better than nongay women. They tended to be more candid and less defensive. They have a high degree of adaptability and often report a sense of freedom.

The following quote by John C. Gonsiorek was made after he had studied all the available research relating to homosexuality and mental illness:

> It is my contention that the issue of whether homosexuality per se is a sign of psychopathology, psychological maladjustment, or disturbance has been answered, and the answer is that it is not. . . . This is not to say that psychologically disturbed homosexuals do not exist; nor does it mean that no homosexuals are disturbed because of their sexuality. Rather, the conclusion is that homosexuality in and of itself bears no necessary relationship to psychological adjustment. This should not be surprising; heterosexuals disturbed because of their sexuality fill many therapists' caseloads.[15]

MYTH #6—GAYS AND LESBIANS ARE FEW AND FAR BETWEEN

Since most gays and lesbians feel they must remain in the closet, no one can give with confidence a precise number of gay people in the American population. Various reliable sources have estimated that 10 percent of the population is exclusively or predominantly lesbian or gay. Other studies claim that the gay population is as low as 3 percent. Even if you take these percentages with skepticism, one can see that an enormous number of Americans (and other nationalities) are homosexual. Consider these figures:

U.S. population (July 1995): 263,000,000 (rounded).
If 10 percent are gay, there are 26,300,000 gay Americans.
If 3 percent are gay, there are 7,890,000 gay Americans.

And the number of parents, siblings, other relatives, and friends of gays is many times greater.

On the average, a classroom full of children will have one to three who are destined to be gay. Two out of twenty parents at any school will have a lesbian or gay child.

Both the 10 percent or the 3 percent categories tell us that lesbians and gays are everywhere. They tell us that their parents are everywhere. All are subject in one way or another to the cruel prejudices of society. As one parent said, "When you attack homosexuality or make fun of gays and lesbians, or think homosexual people should be denied their rights, you are sure to hurt someone you know and love. You're hurting a friend, a neighbor, a cousin, a niece, a nephew, a brother or sister, a son or daughter."

MYTH #7—GAYS AND LESBIANS CHOSE IT AND THEREFORE THEY CAN CHANGE IT

Choice and change are closely interrelated in the public mind. The belief goes: "If gay persons choose to be gay, then they can choose not to be gay. They can change. They do not have to act on their gay feelings. Therefore, all the forces of the society should be brought to bear on gay and lesbian persons to force them into the straight and narrow path of heterosexuality."

On the other hand, if gayness is a natural condition and is essentially impervious to change, then all of the efforts to change sexual orientation are a waste of time and effort. All the rhetoric that condemns gayness is then erroneous thinking. The denial of rights, the cruel jokes, the physical attacks against lesbians and gays are all signs of a society that needs to reexamine its values on this whole issue.

The concept of choice itself is highly ambiguous. It can be used, for example, by people who have denied their homosexuality for years, but finally *acknowledge* or *"choose"* to accept their true sexual identity. That is radically different from the notion, "Oh well, I guess I'll just 'choose' to be homosexual"—as if it were as simple as casually choosing vanilla over strawberry at the ice cream store.

Parents, too, have a major stake in the choice/chan/ versy. Thinking that their child has a choice brings out fears. Many will not stop pressuring their child to conform. The choice/change mind-set also keeps parents from examining their old dreams, from taking the steps necessary to rearrange those dreams, and from accepting their child's right to be different.

Most modern therapists agree that a predominantly gay orientation cannot and should not be changed. Forcing a gay child to "shape up or ship out," no matter how lovingly done, is not an answer.

Most current research supports the belief that behaviors can be chosen, but basic orientation cannot. A person could choose not to act on gayness and to live a celibate life. And some gay people do so, preferring celibacy to the risk of rejection. They can also suppress their homosexuality, deny it, hate themselves for it. They may even choose to live a semblance of a heterosexual life. Experience seems to indicate that this is a recipe for unfulfillment at best, disaster at worst. The obvious conclusion drawn from this controversy is that the whole subject of our heterosexual or homosexual nature is, as yet, incompletely understood.

Once parents examine and discard the choice/change idea, their difficulty in accepting the gayness of their child is greatly eased. The uproar dies down, and everyone finds relief from the sense of danger that accompanies the issue of choice. They begin to see that homosexuality is normal—a bit unusual when viewed from their heterosexual orientation—but basically normal.

MYTH #8—GAYS AND LESBIANS ARE EASY TO IDENTIFY

The vast majority of lesbian and gay people are very much hidden. Howard Brown's book, *Familiar Faces, Hidden Lives,* sums up how most gay and lesbian people live. They are held back by fears of job loss, rejection by families, and a real sense of physical danger.

Some gays and lesbians do choose to let the nongay world know what their sexual orientation is. Out of this group, a very small number reveal their gayness with behavior or dress that fits the commonly held stereotype. These actions say to the world, "I am me. I will not deny my sexual nature. I will handle whatever I have to face."

There is another group of gay people who are easy to identify—those who freely get into the fight for gay rights and come out in all phases of their lives. The benefits they have won for all gay people far outweigh their small number. They have made life easier for everyone associated with the gay community. By refusing to disappear, these activists are forcing society to acknowledge them. They do not accept the oppressive tactics that are being used against them and their brothers and sisters.

Many other gay people choose to be identified in a limited way. They come out to particular groups such as their family or friends or fellow workers. Even this partial coming out challenges the stereotype and lessens society's attack on the homosexual lifestyle. Only the most insensitive people can ridicule or condemn a relative or a good friend or a person they work with every day.

Most of us have been guilty of thinking we can identify gays and lesbians from their outward appearance or behavior. Because we knew some, we assumed we could recognize all. The truth is if all gay people decided to wear a purple hat on a given day, we would be amazed at their numbers. In an article, Letha Scanzoni punctures the smugness of many of us:

> One lesbian told me, "It kills me that people sit around talking stereotypically about gays and don't know they're sitting next to one in church."
>
> Similarly, another woman told of a time when a professional colleague pointed out a stranger on the street and said, "That man is a homosexual. I can spot one anytime, just by looking at them." She recalled thinking, "Oh, if you could only know! You've worked with me for nearly a quarter of a century—and have never guessed my orientation. And because of your anxiety and hostility over this topic, I'll never be able to share this part of myself with you, even though you think of me as your friend."

In another case, a pastor boasted of his ability to detect homosexual persons because "the Holy Spirit bore witness" in his heart whenever a gay person happened on the scene. Yet he hadn't the foggiest notion that his highly esteemed assistant pastor, living celibately, had struggled for years to come to terms with his own homosexual orientation.[16]

MYTH #9—GAY AND LESBIAN PERSONS ARE POOR PARENTS. IT WILL HARM CHILDREN TO LIVE WITH SAME-SEX PARENTS

Most gay people spend a great deal of their early lives trying desperately to fit into the heterosexual version of family life or grieving over their inability to do so. Some marry in the hope that they will somehow not be who they are.

Many gay people, both men and women, express a deep longing for a family of their own. They want not only a long-term, loving, stable relationship, but children as well. Some do have children, either from a previous marriage or by donor insemination, adoption, foster care, or co-parenting.

Until fifteen years ago, there was little research on the psychological health of families headed by a lesbian or gay parent or parents. Much of the recent research has been in response to the needs of the courts. Such research is still in its early stages. Many gay parents are reluctant to participate in studies because it is so easy for them to lose custody or visitation rights.

An excellent paper was published in 1992 by Charlotte J. Patterson, of the University of Virginia, summarizing the results of thirty-five research studies comparing the children in families headed by one or two gay parents with families headed by one or two heterosexual parents.[17] Participants were matched in terms of age, sex, education, economic status, etc. The author drew on seventy-seven other research papers, giving a history of public and legal policy with respect to gay/lesbian parents; the critical sociopsychological factors that contribute (positively or negatively) toward children's mental health; and demographic information about the parents themselves. Patterson's paper is meticulous in its methods and exhaustive in its scope.

The Patterson summary deals with the mental health aspects of child development in the following areas:

> self-esteem and self-concept
> independence
> gender identity, gender role behavior
> sexual orientation (of adolescent or adult children)
> moral judgment
> intelligence
> behavior/emotional problems
> presence or absence of psychiatric disturbance
> risk for sexual abuse by parents or friends of parents
> hyperactivity
> sociability/unsociability

In every case, children of gay/lesbian parents demonstrated no significant difference from children of heterosexual parents, with respect to the above measures of mental health. The incidence of sexual abuse in gay/lesbian families was extremely low.[18]

> Despite long-standing legal presumptions against gay and lesbian parents in many states, despite dire predictions about their children based on well-known theories of psychosocial development, and despite the accumulation of a substantial body of research investigating these issues, not a single study has found children of gay or lesbian parents to be disadvantaged in any significant respect, relative to children of heterosexual parents. Indeed, the evidence to date suggests that home environments provided by gay and lesbian parents are as likely as those provided by heterosexual parents to support and enable children's psychosocial growth.[19]

Existing research evidence provides no justification for denial of parental rights and responsibilities to lesbians and gay men on the basis of their sexual orientation.[20]

Our Own Experience

For some years now, we have known many lesbian women and gay men who are raising children. As educators, all three of the authors have dealt extensively with many types of parents. The gay/lesbian parents we have known demonstrate outstanding parenting skills. Both our observations and the Patterson study show that gay/lesbian parents are every bit as good as heterosexual parents.

MYTH #10—ALL GAY AND LESBIAN PEOPLE ARE OVERSEXED AND INDISCRIMINATELY PROMISCUOUS

Before I found out about my gay son, I had this ridiculous belief that a gay or lesbian would try to get any person, heterosexual or homosexual, to have sex with them. I'm ashamed now that I thought that.

This parent has since found out that gay people have little or no sexual interest in heterosexuals or in indiscriminate sex. Sexuality is not the only focus of their lives any more than it is for heterosexuals.

While promiscuity does exist in the gay community, it is not nearly as extensive as we have been led to believe. There is as much diversity in sexual patterns in the gay community as there is in the heterosexual community. In fact, gay men are much more like nongay men in their sexual activity than they are like lesbian women. Conversely, lesbian women are more like nongay women in their sexual activity than like gay men.

It is quite possible that the promiscuity exhibited by some gay men may be due to the way society treats them. Gay people live in a repressive atmosphere, exploited as scapegoats by homophobic politicians—an atmosphere that fills them with a sense of danger and insecurity. They are often fearful of losing their jobs. They can be forced to move out of their homes. They can be expelled from the armed services. Until 1995 they could be denied security clearance. When faced with the tragedy of AIDS (acquired immune deficiency syndrome), they are told by some religious groups that they

are receiving punishment from God. Their monogamous relationships are not honored legally or socially. Living under this bar-
rage of attacks, some gay people may act in self-destructive ways.

But we have talked to other gay men who have given us a different perspective. They do not see promiscuity in black and white
terms. They say for many gays it is a means of exploration and ad-
venture; a way of giving and getting affection.

The idea of promiscuity is clearly one that troubles most parents. But care should be taken that a double standard not be used
to judge our gay children. Promiscuity and extramarital affairs are
very much present in the heterosexual world.

*I have been thinking about my gay son's sexuality. It was hard to even
let it into my mind. It's really none of my business what he does in bed. I
don't see sex in the same way my children do. I can't even understand all
the ideas my straight children have about sex, much less my gay son's. I've
decided to live and let live. Of course, I can't help but worry about his health.*

MYTH #11—GAYS AND LESBIANS LIVE A LONELY LIFE AND CONTRIBUTE NOTHING TO SOCIETY

The generalized homophobic picture of gay and lesbian life is that
loneliness is pervasive. In truth, gay men and lesbian women live
very much like their nongay counterparts. Many establish long-
term monogamous relationships out of the desire to spend their
lives with one person. David P. McWhirter and Andrew M. Matti-
son in their book, *The Male Couple,* have investigated the lives of
long-term male couples. They found that gay men go through
stages in their lives together, as the problems of learning to adjust
to each other are worked out. These stages are similar to the stages
of heterosexual marriage.

Overall, the gay and lesbian community provides a haven for its
members. There is love and fun and support. There is self-
acceptance and understanding. There is hope and commitment.
All these are qualities that any good community would take pride
in. But the truth is that gay people are often forced to leave their

families and small-town communities in order to find the support offered by big-city gay communities. The homophobia of heterosexual society thus weakens family ties.

We asked a young gay man to talk about the specific ways that the gay culture supports its members and enhances the rest of society. Here are some highlights from his response. His pride and awareness of his own worth are shared by many gays and lesbians.

I think there are some special features in gay community life, but I wouldn't want people to assume that all gay people have to fit them. We have to be careful about generalizations. Although they can contain important truths, they can also limit the vision of who gay people are.

There is a lot of humor among gay people. There is a sense of playfulness and revelry. You can see some of it in the gay pride parades when people dress up in colorful and humorous costumes. And it's there in daily life too. There's a whole satirical tradition called camp that includes a secret language that people on the inside can appreciate. Words like butch, dyke, queen, sissy, fairy, queer *which in the straight world are used in a derogatory way, may be used by gay people in a humorous, appreciative way.*

Then there is also a serious side in the gay style, a sense of the tragic aspects of life, which is very deep and rich among gay and lesbian people. Part of this is because of the suffering in our homophobic society, but also I think gays and lesbians are more sensitive. I know that's the stereotype, but I think it is true that as a group we are more tuned into emotional life, spiritual life, close communication, how people feel, and the price that is paid for ignoring these feelings.

In terms of contributions to the broader culture, I think that the arts and the nurturing professions are two expressions of this greater sensitivity. A lot of great writers, performers, and artists have been gay, partly because we have a very pronounced sense of the sorrow of life. As a group, there is a great depth of understanding. If you could remove all of the books, plays, and movies by gays, the gay actors, dancers, clowns, animal trainers, nurses, teachers, social workers, psychologists, therapists, you'd see a lot of blank spaces in American artistic and work life.

There is a strong sense of solidarity in both the gay and lesbian communities. We do an incredible amount of taking care of each other. If straight people could open their eyes to this, it could be an example for them.

We have always been active in social and political movements. Someone could write a book documenting the participation of gay people in the civil rights movement, the anti-war movement, the farm worker movement, the anti-imperialist movement. We participate out of proportion to our numbers.

In various and sundry ways, we nudge the society along. I think that's partly because many of us are not as bound by large families. We can afford to be catalysts for change. We have more freedom to be innovators. Because gay people have often been excluded from mainstream American life, they have had to live by their wits, create their own resources, and develop the courage to be their own persons.

MYTH #12—AIDS IS A MALE HOMOSEXUAL DISEASE

Facts:

The World Health Organization reported in February 1995 that, worldwide, 50 percent of all new HIV infections are in women—almost all of them heterosexual. Only a tiny percent of lesbians are infected.

In Africa, six women now are infected for every four men. The World Health Organization also reports that across the globe 7 to 8 million women of childbearing age are HIV positive, including 5.5 million in Africa and 1.3 million in Asia.

This terrible toll is due in part to religious teachings which hold that the use of condoms is a sin.

NEW EVIDENCE REFUTES DISCREDITED MYTHS AND UNTRUE STEREOTYPES

The myths and distorted stereotypes about gay people have been further eroded by recent findings of historical studies and scientific research.

The religious right charges that gay people are demented perverts and mentally ill, but this charge becomes comical when we consider the creative genius and varied accomplishments of men and women that historical research or modern journalism has revealed as homosexual: Michelangelo, Leonardo da Vinci, Gertrude Stein, Willa Cather, Dag Hammarskjöld, Bayard Rustin, Jane Addams, Barbara Jordan, Hans Christian Andersen, W. H. Auden, Leonard Bernstein, Peter Ilyich Tchaikovsky, Cole Porter, Tennessee Williams, James Baldwin, Walt Whitman, Virginia Woolf, May Swenson, T. E. Lawrence, John Maynard Keynes, Pope Julius III, Susan B. Anthony, Frederick the Great, Richard the Lionhearted, Queen Christina of Sweden, and King James I, who sponsored the translation of the Bible that bears his name.[21] In recent years sports champions Martina Navratilova and Greg Louganis, actor Ian McKellen, business leader David Geffen, and state legislators Deborah Glick and Sheila Kuehl have identified themselves as gay. The current U.S. Congress includes three openly gay Representatives: Barney Frank and Gerry Studds (Democrats, Massachusetts) and Steve Gunderson (Republican, Wisconsin), while the Canadian Parliament has one openly gay member, Svend Robinson.

On the current scene, debate still rages around the question of whether homosexuality is a given—perhaps biologically determined—or if it is a deliberate choice.

The final word as to "cause" remains unknown, but new scientific studies have given support to the hypothesis that biological, genetic, and hormonal factors are significantly involved. Recent research has thrown new light on homosexuality, even as it has revealed the enormous complexity involved in explaining sexuality of any kind. There is no "magic bullet" answer to questions such as: What is homosexuality? What causes homosexuality? Years of research will be required to get more adequate answers than those available now.

Yet in the past dozen years important advances have been made in biological research where only conjecture was available before. Two of the respected pioneers in studying the relationship of biological factors to homosexuality are Simon LeVay, formerly a neuroscientist at the Salk Institute for Biological Studies and now the director of the Institute of Gay and Lesbian Education in West

Hollywood, California, and Dean Hamer, formerly of the Biochemical Laboratories of the National Cancer Institute and now a geneticist at the National Institutes of Health. Their work has discredited much of the loose, politically motivated rhetoric about homosexuality.

The work of LeVay and Hamer is very important—and very technical, not easy for lay readers to understand. Fortunately for us a detailed review of the studies by LeVay and Hamer appeared in the July 1995 issue of *The New York Review of Books.* The reviewer was Richard Horton, M.D., editor of *The Lancet,* an influential medical journal with readers throughout the world that reports on scientific investigations in general medicine and clinical research.[22]

LeVay's research won international attention when he reported his study of autopsies of gay and straight men and women. He found that a tiny region in the center of the brain—the interstitial nucleus of the anterior hypothalamus ($INAH_3$)—was, on average, substantially smaller among nineteen gay men than among sixteen heterosexual men; it was about the same size as the $INAH_3$ of the women studied. This was a stunning discovery that confirmed the hypothesis that the hypothalamus had a role in sexual behavior.

LeVay, however, true to the canons of scientific research, argued for caution. He had shown that human sexual preference "is amenable to study at the biological level,"[23] but he warned that it was impossible to determine if the anatomical differences between gay and straight men were a cause or a consequence of their sexual orientation.

Meanwhile Dean Hamer then at the National Cancer Institute chose a different strategy in an attempt to explore the relationship between biological factors and male sexual behavior. In a painstaking search for a genetic connection Hamer studied the rates of homosexuality in male relatives of seventy-six men who identified themselves as gay. He found that the incidence of homosexual orientation, in this population, was strikingly higher than in a sample of heterosexuals who had no history of homosexuality in their families. In addition, the gay men in Hamer's study were, to a statistically significant degree, related to the other homosexual males in their families through their mothers and her sisters. This finding suggests that a gene or genes on the X chromosome (which men inherit only from their mothers) plays a role in determining sexual orientation. Hamer then studied forty pairs of gay brothers and found that thirty-three of the pairs had the same, unusual "DNA markers" on their X chromosomes, another scientific finding that strengthens the hypothesis that there is a genetic basis for homosexuality.

These studies suggest tantalizing possibilities linking homosexuality with genetic, hormonal, and other biological factors. In fact, Dr. Richard Horton wrote in his review of the research by LeVay and Hamer that:

> Taken together the scientific papers of both LeVay and Hamer . . . make a forceful but by no means definitive case for the view that biological and genetic factors have an important, perhaps even decisive, part in determining sexual preference among males.[24]

Both Levay and Hamer acknowledge the complexity in trying to trace DNA connections to sexual orientation and behavior. But they are doggedly determined to stay with the methods of the scientific research tradition.

As we go to press, there are new reports on the most recent work of Dean Hamer and his colleague Angela Pattatucci and their team at the National Institutes of Health. *The Advocate* magazine, in its June 11, 1996, issue, reports on a new book by Chandler Burr, *A Separate Creation: The Search for the Biological Origins of Sexual Orientation*. Among Burr's comments:

1. The groundbreaking Kinsey scale of the 1950s may be outdated by the Hamer team's investigations.

2. The Hamer team's research leans toward the idea that sexual orientation (heterosexual or homosexual) may be determined by a single gene, as yet not isolated.

3. One of Hamer's colleagues who preferred to remain anonymous said that more evidence is needed, but "if you look where the data is going, there is not much question" that it supports a genetic hypothesis.

The courageous studies of scientists like Hamer who pursue the truth wherever the evidence leads them are at odds with the beliefs of the conservative Religious Right. The American public now is confronted with a critical choice: (1) to be guided by the results of scientific inquiry or (2) to choose to stay with the antigay teachings of ancient religious writings.

THE DAMAGE OF UNTRUE MYTHS

The injustice our children have to face as a result of untrue myths is extensive. During the past ten years new research findings and media decisions to let gay people and their parents appear on television have given viewers accurate information about homosexuals, thus breaking down negative stereotypes. They have also triggered homophobic reactions and rage by those on the far right who feel that moves toward acceptance will undermine the "divine" tenets of their ideology. Right-wing politicians and religious leaders appeal to those who hold the ancient attitudes. They have found that antigay campaigns can fill their coffers and support their ambitions for power. We have faith, however, that in the long run the truth will win out over the angry dissemination of discredited myths.

NOTES FOR CHAPTER TWO

1. Irving Bieber et al., eds., *Homosexuality: A Psychoanalytic Study* (New York: Basic Books, 1962).

2. For an analysis and critique, see two studies: William Paul et al., eds., *Homosexuality: Social, Psychological and Biological Issues* (Beverly Hills, Calif.: Sage Publications, Inc., 1982), pp. 68–69, 81–82, 128–129, and Noretta Koertge, ed., *Nature and Causes of Homosexuality: A Philosophic and Scientific Inquiry* (New York: The Haworth Press, 1982), p. 61.

3. Alan P. Bell, Martin S. Weinberg, and Sue K. Hammersmith, *Sexual Preference: Its Development in Men and Women* (Bloomington: Indiana University Press, 1981).

4. Ibid., p. 9.

5. Ibid., p. 238. (The breakdown of the number of years spent in the study was provided in a lecture by Martin Weinberg.)

6. Ibid., pp. 191–192. (Italics in text.)

7. Ibid., pp. 183–184.

8. Ibid., p. 188.

9. Ibid., p. 185.

10. Ibid., pp. 187–188.

11. Ibid., p. 185.

12. William Paul et al., eds., "Results of Psychological Testing on Homosexual Populations," pp. 73–74, *Homosexuality: Social, Psychological and Biological Issues.* Copyright © 1982 by Sage Publications, Inc., Beverly Hills.

13. Evelyn A. Hooker, "The Adjustment of the Male Overt Homosexual," *Journal of Projective Techniques,* 21, no. 1 (1957), pp. 17–31.

14. Mark Freedman, "Stimulus-Response: Homosexuals May Be Healthier Than Straights," *Psychology Today,* 8, no. 10 (March 1975), pp. 28–32.

15. Paul, op. cit., pp. 78–79. Reprinted by permission of Sage Publications, Inc.

16. Letha Dawson Scanzoni, "Putting a Face on Homosexuality," *The Other Side,* Issue 149 (February 1984), p. 8. Reprinted by permission from *The Other Side* magazine, 300 W. Apsley Street, Philadelphia, Pa. 19144.

17. Charlotte J. Patterson, "Children of Lesbian and Gay Parents," *Child Development,* vol. 63 (1992), pp. 1025–1042, published by the Society for Research in Child Development, Inc. We are grateful to Mollie M. Wallick, Ph.D., Professor, Department of Psychiatry, School of Medicine, Louisiana State University, for calling this article to our attention during a seminar she led at a P-FLAG national convention, October 1993.

18. Ibid., p. 1034.

19. Ibid., p. 1036.

20. Ibid., p. 1037.

21. See also "Prominent Gay People Throughout History" in D. Wallickinsky and A. Wallace, *The People's Almanac Presents The Book of Lists* (New York: William Morrow, 1977).

22. Richard Horton, M.D., "Is Homosexuality Inherited?" *The New York Review of Books* (July 13, 1995), pp. 36–41.

23. Simon LeVay, "A Difference in Hypothalamic Structure Between Heterosexual and Homosexual Men," *Science* (August 30, 1991), pp. 1034–1037. For a review of these studies and the issues they raise, see *Why Ask Why? Addressing the Research on Homosexuality and Society* (Washington, D.C.: P-FLAG Publications, 1995).

24. Horton, op. cit., p. 37.

*Healing can happen if you
receive two things: knowledge
and human support.
The best available tool is the
"grief cycle," but for most people
the cycle will not be complete
unless they share their grief with
someone who has been through a
similar experience.*[1]

■

THREE

■

COMMUNICATING
WITH OTHERS

Books by careful researchers and by people honestly knowledgeable about homosexuality can help parents in many important ways. But reading was not enough for most of us. We had to talk out our grief and fears.

Honest talk was the key ingredient. Healing accelerated as we shared our feelings with people who were willing to listen, willing to understand the hurt, and willing to tell of their own feelings. This help came from a variety of sources—a good friend, our own gay child, other parents of gays and lesbians, other gays and lesbians, and/or the right type of counselor.

TELLING A FRIEND

Sharing our hurt with a close friend can be a great source of comfort.

I called my best friend and told her. She said, "What do you want me to say to you?" I answered that I wanted her to tell me she loved me and that everything was going to be okay. At that time I needed to have a sense of belonging to someone. I needed to feel that I was not a failure, that I had tried.

And she said, "Of course I love you. Don's sexuality has nothing to do with our relationship." She really pulled it together for me. She understood what I was going through.

GETTING HELP FROM OUR OWN CHILD

Some of us found another source of help—a source even closer to home—our own gay son or lesbian daughter. Many parents gratefully told of the help they received from their children.

I didn't know much when I first found out. So I started coming up with all these questions for my son. I was fortunate because Don would always answer them. Sometimes he didn't like the questions and would laugh at them, but he always gave me truthful answers no matter how silly he thought they were. That helped me a great deal.

I remember once I even asked him if he hung around in the restrooms at the park. He said, "Only when I have to urinate." That was the answer I needed. I had so many bad thoughts because of what I was reading in the paper. Talking to Don and finding out how he felt took away these scary ideas. He gave me books too. I wanted to know. It was important for me to know.

■

I think my relationship with Robin is closer now. Before there was always this barrier. Now I know precisely where I stand. Our relationship is open, and we can talk about everything.

We always did have a good relationship when she was growing up. But it took me time before I could talk about her lesbianism without getting hysterical. Then there was a period when I never brought it up to her, and she never brought it up to me. Now I can even joke with her and tease her a little bit. I think that's a real sign that I have accepted it.

■

I made some efforts to talk more with Jerry. I was pretty pointed in the things I asked him, because I really didn't know much about homosexuality.

Anytime Jerry came home he would explain his feelings, and then my husband and I could see it a little more clearly through his eyes. Sometimes we would write him. We would even call him on the phone. He was the one who had the experience. We did not. We were the fledglings, the learners. He was the teacher.

■

Finally, after several months, I said to my son, "There have been many things on my mind, and one of the things I'm wondering is how can I be supportive in this? What do you want me to do?" And he said, "Nothing special—just whatever you feel is right. If you're uncomfortable about anything, ask me any questions. Talk to me about whatever is bothering you."

One of my initial reactions was "He's going to be so badly hurt when he's rejected." But he hasn't been. He was totally prepared for the fact that certain people who were his friends suddenly aren't anymore. He doesn't care. He feels that it's their problem, not his.

Some of his healthy attitude rubbed off on me, because I had been so afraid of other people's opinions. Now I find I no longer care what people think.

LEARNING FROM OTHER GAYS AND LESBIANS

There is another dimension that plays a critical role: meeting and getting to know other lesbians and gay men. In the beginning, the only gay or lesbian that we *know* we know is our own child. We are afraid that if we meet other homosexuals, then we'll discover that all those scary stories we've heard are true. It takes time to realize that having access to gay people in natural situations is a vital resource for getting in touch with the truths about gayness. We found that our fears were unfounded.

All the information you can get, plus support from other parents, isn't enough to convince you at a deeper level that lesbians and gays are okay as people. It isn't until you meet gay people, and share with them something about your lives, that big changes begin to occur.

Without meeting gay people you can't really shake the homophobia. When we talk together in our rap groups, we share a common pain, sometimes including tears. Then a bond gradually builds. The stereotypes just fall away. It doesn't matter that Joan is lesbian and Bill is gay. As we grow together, our fondness for one another grows. We become willing to stand up for each other against the hurts of a hostile world.

■

At one Parents FLAG meeting I was talking to a young lesbian, and I said, "Just think of all the hurt my daughter is going to go through." She said, "But that's your definition of what hurt is. That may not be the way your daughter or I would react." That helped ease some of my fears.

LEARNING FROM COUNSELORS

Some of us found help from counselors. It is important, however, that parents be careful in their selection of a counselor or therapist because many of them are not up-to-date about homosexuality.

Even though the American Psychiatric Association has removed homosexuality from its list of mental disorders, and the American Psychological Association and the American Nurses Association have called for an end to discrimination against homosexuality, we are still in a period of transition. Too many therapists hang onto the "desirability" of heterosexuality. Such professionals do damage to gay men, lesbians, and their parents. We urge those parents who seek professional help to ask what the therapist believes about gayness. Do not go to someone who is negative or who views homosexuality as something that should or could be changed.

First, I went to a counselor at our group health center. She was a warm, motherly person, and with a gentle smile, she told me, "I think it's just a phase. He is probably in a rebellious stage, trying to get your attention. Keep contact with him, and he'll probably grow out of it." That's just what I wanted to hear; but as I look back on it, I see that although she had good intentions, she was really as ignorant on the subject as I was. Her training had taught her that being gay was misbehavior or arrested development.

Later I joined a therapy group with a counselor who had a very different attitude. One of her first questions was "Are you and Jack blaming each other?" I said we weren't. I had a lot of confused thoughts at the time. She assured me that we need not get into blaming someone; that homosexuality was just part of the human condition. Chris could live a happy, productive life. Our job was to learn to live with it in nondestructive ways.

■

I started looking for a counselor who knew the facts about homosexuality and could make me feel better. After the exhilaration of finally meeting with one, I experienced some depression. I began to realize that although my "head trip" had been very effective and intense, I had not really dealt with the grief. Through continued help from a skilled counselor, I worked through much grief.

There are both gay and nongay therapists who have well-grounded knowledge about homosexuality, and who can help parents become clearly informed about the subject. With these therapists, parents can get valuable help in dealing with their feelings and clarifying their attitudes.

I was in a counseling group when Barbara told us, and that was a big help. I had been fighting depression, with terrible feelings about being a failure as a teacher. I felt I might not be able to go on. When I got the news about Barbara, it just felt like the last straw.

Fortunately for me, the therapist and group members were nonjudgmental about gayness. I got support when I needed it.

It took me some years to work through different phases to the point where I now feel good about Barbara and myself, and I can go out and work for gay rights. But the group therapy at that early time helped me through one of the hardest times. I was lucky.

RECEIVING SUPPORT FROM OTHER PARENTS OF GAY PEOPLE

Over and over again, we heard parents say that finding the way to other parents of gay people or to a parent support group became an important turning point. It is much easier to move away from an awful sense of loneliness if we share it with someone who has experienced the same thing. It's a relief to discover that these other parents are so much like ourselves—they share the common goal of learning to understand themselves and their children.

I was sick, and a special friend came to see me, bringing with her—believe it or not—some of her homemade chicken soup. My pain about Linda was so great I could not hide it any longer. The hour that followed was filled with tears and anguish. When I finished, she said quietly, "I think I understand. That is our situation too. Our son is gay. I know how it feels, but if it is any comfort to you, it won't seem so painful two years from now."

At last I had someone with whom I could share. And what a difference! That was the first step toward healing. Also the first step toward entering into the nameless world where probably one in ten human beings suffers as a result of being so little understood and so maligned.

■

I had read about a parents-of-gays group in an Ann Landers column. I wrote a letter to the post office box listed in the column. It was the hard-

est thing I've ever done in my life. For all I knew, the parents' group was some kooky organization. I had all sorts of thoughts that maybe they would put our name in the papers or something like that. But I wrote that letter anyway, because we were desperate to talk to somebody. We were eager to meet other people who were willing to admit they had a homosexual child.

The other parents at the first meeting had been where we were. It was comforting to know that we were not going through this alone. It was the sense of a common bond—that they were all trying to accept it or tolerate it or cope with it—that was just comforting. It did something for us. We could face the world again. I wouldn't take anything for the people we've met in the group.

■

We felt we had no one, no one to talk to except each other, and we had exhausted the subject. When we finally got to the parents' group, it was so good to be with other people and exchange experiences and ideas and thoughts and the pain that you feel at first. And then we began to go through the different levels, toward acceptance.

I don't think I had been in that first meeting very long when I made a commitment to myself—that I would keep coming back. It was easy for me to see that this wasn't a place where people came to look and point at each other. Instead, they came to try to help one another with their problems.

■

Andy was only seven when his father died, and he was the youngest child. I thought about how I brought him up after that, and I can't think how I could have done it any other way. I also took large doses of hormones before he was born, because I'd had a series of miscarriages previously. Yet in the support group I'm the only one who had had these experiences. It proved to me that those things didn't cause the homosexuality. I'm forever grateful that there was a group to go to when I needed it. Parents need to know there is someone else with the same problems.

■

I have a great time at the parents' meeting. I've been thinking about that lately and decided that it is our sharing of the tough things that brings us closer. We can be ourselves, and we can talk about the part of ourselves that is vulnerable. We're having fun at the same time. The group has a purpose, and there are nice people in it. When we are together, we can be who we are and not fear being condemned. I feel that I can say almost anything about myself in that group. It's comfortable.

The following interchange between Virginia and Fran occurred during an interview conducted for this book. We present it at some length because it reveals the mutual aid that can develop between parents of gay people who have built trust in each other.

Virginia: *Why don't you start out by telling how your son came out to you?*

Fran: *It was about five years ago when Ed wrote Hal and me a letter. Hal is my other son. Ed just wrote that he was gay. He said that he had felt from very early childhood that he was different. He had had sex with girls, but it was distasteful to him. He knew that it could never be any other way but homosexual for him.*

He told me that he had always felt conflict between us and that he hoped his telling me would clear it up. That feeling is all gone now. We both understand how and why there was a strain in our relationship.

I had always suspected, even from early childhood. His father was overseas until Ed was a year old. The first time he saw Ed he said, "He walks like a girl." Ed was always effeminate and got along better with girls as a young boy in grade school. He played with girls and was always teased by the boys. It wasn't until high school, when he got into drama, that he was able to relate to both sexes.

It was at this time that his father and I went through a divorce. I was going to move from California to the Midwest, and Ed begged me not to. (She cries.) I knew I wouldn't get through this.

Virginia: *It really does upset you a lot.*

Fran: *Ed begged me not to move because he said he just knew he couldn't get along here in the Midwest. So we did stay another year. He graduated, and he had good relationships with his peers for the first time in his life. Now he's in California where he has lots of friends.*

Virginia: *You still feel a sense of loss?*

Fran: *Very much so.* (She cries.) *Although we can't say why he is a homosexual, I believe he was born that way. I think true homosexuals are all born that way. Because of our religion, I always hope and pray that he will change. But I really don't expect it. You know, I'm very proud of the way he conducts himself. His homosexuality is just a very small part of him.*

Virginia: *It seemed to touch on something very deep when you started talking about this a while ago.*

Fran: *Well, I know what he has to go through as a gay man. It's a hard life for him. I think he would be a good family man if he could marry and have children. He has even said that he hopes he can figure some way to have children. That's how much he wants a family. I would certainly like to have normal family relationships with grandchildren. This part of it is a real heartbreaker.*

Virginia: *Is that what bothers you the most? The lack of an accepted family situation?*

Fran: *That and the fact that he has to be in California. I miss him, but he can't live a normal life here. I would like for us all to be together like other families. But I can't be open with the rest of my family about his situation.*

Virginia: *It's pretty lonely.*

Fran: *Yes. It hurts not being able to communicate. I feel like I'm always leading a double life, always on guard. I guess I'm in the closet more than he is. The only place I can talk about him is in the parents' group. That group helps me more than anything else. Talking to the other parents proved to me that I wasn't weird because this has happened. It wasn't because of the bad marriage.*

Virginia: *It sounds as if you feel very uncomfortable about this double life you're describing.*

Fran: *I always do. I think the big hang-up is religion. I still worry about his acceptance in the church.*

Virginia: *It's hard for you to accept what the church says knowing how he has to live.*

Fran: *Right.*

Virginia: *You're deeply religious and you feel pulled both ways.*

Fran: *I was at one time. Now I'm beginning to wonder about the church and all its rules. I don't really feel like they've helped people on an indi-*

vidual basis. What happens to me doesn't seem to really matter. Am I making any sense?

Virginia: *You're making a lot of sense. What would you like from the church?*

Fran: *Some understanding.* (She cries.) *I feel really persecuted in the church. I just think the priests don't really understand what people go through. If you try and give it your best shot and don't make it, you shouldn't be persecuted.*

Virginia: *So, you feel like there are a couple of areas where you have not made it—a gay son and a divorce?*

Fran: *I did the best I could in both areas. I know I did. I think I should be excused. You can only take so much. You can't do any more. You can't force people to fit into a mold. I'm going to try to be as happy as I can be; I want Ed to be as happy as he can be. But I can't make church members and family members see that.*

Virginia: *That sounds strong. Do you feel strong when you say that?*

Fran: *Right. But, of course, I couldn't make them understand because I've never really said it before.* (They laugh.)

Virginia: *Church doctrine changes, Fran. The doctrine of any church is only an interpretation of the Word. The doctrine changes as society changes.*

Fran: *It's kind of backward right now.*

Virginia: *There's a minority group of people in your religion who view being gay in a pretty good light. You can choose to believe the negative view or you can choose to believe the positive. I feel better when I look at my son's gayness in as positive a light as possible.*

Fran: *You seem to know just what I need. I always feel better when I talk with you and the other people in the group. It just doesn't stay with me long enough.*

Virginia: *It's no wonder. You're all by yourself.*

Fran: *I can't even talk with Hal about it. He doesn't agree with it either.*

Virginia: *It's not a matter of agreeing or disagreeing when you really get down to it, Fran. It's a matter of "he is or he is not." Ed is gay and can't be otherwise.*

Fran: *I know that in my head. Yet sometimes I find it difficult to be around Ed for very long. His ways are just different from what I'm used to. He's different from what you'd expect of a traditional male.*

Virginia: *Is he effeminate?*

Fran: *Yes. That kind of tears me up. It's hard for me to agree with that part of him.*

Virginia: *Would you want to change him?*

Fran: *He's always been rather uninhibited. He does little things that are unusual, like bleaching his hair and talking to the animals at the zoo. I watched him do that, and it embarrassed me. You don't see many people standing around talking to the animals.* (They laugh.)

But afterward I felt guilty. I love him, and yet I'm bothered by some of his actions. I wouldn't want to change him. He is the way he is. If I could change him, he wouldn't be the same boy.

Virginia: *Have you ever thought about the fact that at the time you found out he was gay, you lost him in a special kind of way? It happened about the same time you lost the sense of security that went with being married. You also lost your husband. You really had a mass of losses, all at the same time.*

Fran: *That's what part of this feeling I have is all about. It took me a year to tell my parents that I was divorced. I didn't want them to worry.*

I never told my mother about Ed's being gay. I'm afraid that it would be devastating for her. She's seventy-eight, and I doubt she could accept it. I don't talk about it anywhere except at our group. I have to take another step if I'm going to talk about Ed to my family or in public.

Virginia: *It takes a while, Fran. Don't push yourself too soon. Are you beginning to feel that it's time for you to take another step?*

Fran: *Yes, I think so. If I could do it without crying.*

Virginia: *Try to be whatever you are at the moment. Because what you are is a super person. If you feel like crying, then I don't think you've cried enough.*

Fran: *But it's been five years.* (Her voice breaks.)

Virginia: *Feeling okay didn't come easy for me. I had the same kind of struggle. It gets even lonelier if you think other people are doing better than you are. It has been hard for me too. There's nothing wrong with you because you're still struggling. I just want you to know you don't have to struggle alone. Call me whenever you feel upset.*

Fran: *I'd like to get to the place where I wouldn't be crying when I talk about Ed's being gay. I'd like to be able to talk about it like you do. I want to be open.*

Virginia: *It is nice. I was surprised at how much better I felt after I became more open. I had thought it was better to stay behind a wall. But it wasn't.*

Fran, you seem to be on a treadmill, and you've been on that treadmill for a long time. And you sound as if you're tired of it.

Fran: *Yes! I'm a pretty open person. I hate to have all these secrets. I want to be able to just say what I think and feel.*

In the back of my mind I keep Mother as a big excuse to hold myself in. Oh, I don't know if that is all it is, but we have always kept everything from my mother. If I hurt her in any way, I might not ever forgive myself.

But when Ed was here, he asked why I didn't tell everyone. I told him I just couldn't. It's really up to him whether he wants to tell them or not.

Virginia: *It's also partly up to you though, isn't it?*

Fran: *Yes, right. I guess my mother is more my responsibility than his. I worry about how she would accept it and what it would do to her.*

Virginia: *Can you really expect your family to accept Ed's being gay better than you have? They might not accept it at first, but later they may change—as you have.*

Fran: *My whole family has the same Christian background. I know they would have the same feelings I have had.*

Virginia: *I'm just saying that even if you tell somebody and they don't approve, you can understand where their feelings come from.*

Fran: *When you tell somebody, Virginia, what kind of atmosphere do you tell them in?*

Virginia: *As I have changed my own feelings, I have told about my son in different ways. At first I cried. I got the comfort that I needed. Later I was more matter-of-fact about it because I wanted to educate people to the fact that I had a gay son, and that I didn't want to hear any gay jokes. Whatever you're feeling at the time is the way you tell about it. At least it was for me.*

Fran: *It takes a lot to speak up. Right now I can only come out in the group because there aren't many Catholics there. And the ones who are there agree with me.*

If I spoke out in my own territory or my own family, I'd be clobbered. I'll probably just sit and be a quiet little mouse like I always have been.

Virginia: *Fran, there is inside of you a very articulate, a very capable, a very strong person who is having a hard time keeping quiet.*

Fran: *Thank you. I'm glad you got that on tape.* (She laughs.)

Virginia: *I'll tell you what—there is a question I'd like to ask you that I think might be interesting. I'll ask it and then you can answer or not. Knowing that homosexuality is probably biological for most gay people, would you have treated Ed any differently than you did?*

Fran: *No, I don't see how I could have. I always felt that what I did at the time was the best thing I could do.*

Virginia: *You thought it through?*

Fran: *Right.*

Virginia: *Didn't try to make him into something he wasn't?*

Fran: *No, I always tried to help him be himself. There were times when he was playing with the girls that I would, you know, try to get him to play with the boys. But he just didn't fit in. It wasn't until high school when the boys were switching to the girls that he was switching to the boys.* (They laugh.) *You can't change something that strong. For the same reason, when I discovered that he was left-handed I never tried to change him to using his right hand. I knew it just wouldn't be him.*

Virginia: *So early on you accepted him for what he was?*

Fran: *Right, yes. It's something that was just meant to be.*

It is clear from the talk between Virginia and Fran that religion can be one of the most disturbing concerns of parents of gays. We heard this concern expressed so often that we decided to investigate the religious issues more closely.

NOTE FOR CHAPTER THREE

1. Rev. Kenneth Czillinger, *Newsletter* (March 1983), American Association of Retired People.

If we as Christians are going to minister to gay people in Christ's name, we first must stop viewing homosexual orientation and homosexual persons in the abstract. We must allow the subject to become personalized to us. . . .

As we stop keeping homosexuality at a distance, as an abstract, and as we see it up close, with a face, something happens to us. We begin to see we are dealing with real human beings made in God's image. And we begin to feel the pain of bearing a stigma and experiencing the oppression and fear as though it were happening to us.[1]

∎

F O U R

∎

RELIGIOUS
THINKING IN
TRANSITION

*S*ome people don't want to understand. And there are many unqualified moral judges sitting in a lot of church pews. It has been a great comfort that Jesus said nothing about this issue. But he did say a lot about judging.

∎

The minister quoted scripture and said that the homosexual lifestyle is a perversion according to Christian biblical principles. "It is a very damaging way of life. Remember Corinthians: 'Do not be deceived; neither the immoral, nor idolators, nor homosexuals, nor thieves, nor the greedy, nor drunkards, nor revilers, nor robbers will inherit the kingdom of God.' " (I Corinthians 6:9)

Will homosexuals go to hell? There is no doubt that for a sizable number of parents that is a real and distressing question. For many of them anxiety about religion is the source of some of their most painful feelings. Questions about this issue need to be resolved if parents are to be at peace with their child's homosexuality.

The statements at the opening of this chapter are examples of the range of attitudes present in the religious communities. Many parents are under the spell of fundamentalist ideas such as those expressed by the minister in the third paragraph. But new attitudes are emerging that challenge the ancient rejections.

We begin with comments from our parents that show the fear and pain, confusion and anger, that welled up in them as they compared the goodness of their gay child with the condemning attitudes.

When I first found out, I gave up every thought of religion. I wondered how God could possibly do this to Tim. He already had the handicap of deafness and had learned to cope with it. I would go to the basement, and I would cuss and denounce God. I felt just terrible. I had this horrible black cloud hanging over me. I would shake my fist and cry, "How can you do this to me? How can you do this to Tim? Why does he have to have this on top of his deafness?" Nobody could hear me because I was down in my basement. I really had a rough time.

When I finally discussed it with my other son, I told him, "I don't believe in God. God couldn't do that. I'll never go to church again. I'll never believe—never, never, never."

All the time I was hating God. One day I took one of my little religious statues and broke it. "I'll never have you in my house again. I'll never pray to you again." My husband, Paul, would say, "Now, Mom, you know God didn't have anything to do with it."

I was in this horrible condition for about six weeks. Because I was afraid I'd start to cry, I didn't want to talk to anybody, didn't want anybody to come around or anything. Then things started to get better. But for a while, because of our upbringing in a little country town, we sure were hurt. There's no question about that. Something like being gay was completely taboo in our town. I mean gays were outcasts. But now we know that they're outcasts in the big cities too.

■

Pretty soon after Don came out to me, he was interviewed by a reporter from the paper. The article appeared—with a picture—on page two of the Sunday paper. It identified Don and a friend of his as professed homosexuals. There it was, the fact that my son was gay, before God and everybody.

All my kids have graduated from Catholic schools, and my youngest was in eighth grade at the time. It was important to me that my kids attend Catholic schools, but because I raised them alone, it was hard for me to get up the money. I had this deal with the priest that when I got my income tax check, I would pay the tuition.

But that year I received letters from the school saying I was delinquent. I called the priest and said, "Father, I keep getting these letters, and I want to know what is going on."

He hesitated, then finally said, "Maybe you'd better come up here, and we'll talk about it." When I went over, Father sat there and stammered. The more he stammered, the redder he got. Finally he said, "Rumor has it that Don condones the homosexual way of life. I can remember that he used to be such a good boy. He used to come to mass every day."

*And I said to him, "Father, that's no rumor. He is homosexual, and he's still a good boy. He still goes to mass every day. His sexuality has nothing to do with how good he is. I walked in here because it was important for my daughter to stay in this school. But if this is the kind of Christianity that you're teaching, it is not what I want my child to be subjected to."
I left. I felt good about standing up for Don, but I felt apart from my church. I had been so active through the years, and to be treated like this hurt.*

■

I went through a period when I could not accept the fact that there was a God. Because if there was a God and a divinely ordered universe, and if homosexuality was wrong, then God didn't order the universe too well. If Rick wasn't okay, and if homosexuality wasn't okay, then there was something wrong with God for letting Rick be the way he was. Why should God put people on earth to be horribly persecuted? I felt I didn't need to look up to a God who would let that happen.

Later I directed my belligerence to church people and their narrow-mindedness. Now I don't feel I have to go along with any organized religion if they're doing things I don't think are conducive to worshipping God. I can find God just sitting quietly by myself. I just can't force myself to go and sit with people who feel bad about my son.

◼

The last time Robin was home from college, my husband, Ron, and I were talking about this religious thing. He was brought up Catholic, and I was not. And he feels that one of the main functions of a marriage is to bear children.

This is the second marriage for both of us. I don't know what he thinks about his sons going out and siring babies out of wedlock and living with people, and so forth. I wasn't about to get into that.

But the other night he was saying that one reason he's having trouble accepting Robin's lesbianism is because to him the purpose of a union is to procreate. And she will not be procreating. So I guess from his stand-point, with his upbringing as a Catholic, it presents more of a problem.

I'm not into Catholicism at all. And the procreation doesn't bother me one bit. I know a lot of people who are married and not having children. What's the difference if you're married and not having children, or if you're living with someone and into having children? You can hardly call them sinful.

◼

I was watching a television show where a minister was saying that gays were an abomination. He mentioned several verses from scripture to prove it and held up a Bible. I sat there glued to my chair for a while. That man doesn't know my son, but he used a biblical one-liner to show his hate. A chill ran down my spine as I thought about my son's being made into a "nonperson" in the name of God.

When I used to read about the Nazis in Germany who were so horrible to the Jewish people, I'd think, "Thank God we're not like that in America." But as I listened to that minister, I wasn't so sure. I thought, "What if more and more people get stirred up by people like him! Could there be a *bloodbath against lesbians and gays here?" For a few minutes I was filled with terror. I had to get up and vacuum the rugs to get my mind off of it.*

I don't really think it could happen here—surely not. I have to think that there are enough fair-minded people in this country who would object.

RELIGIOUS THINKING IN TRANSITION

We can see from these comments that parents take it for granted that their religious leaders and associates will condemn homosexuality. But other parents have used their fears as a spur to explore the changes that are now going on. They have found more diversity than they expected.

My wife, our son, and I were on a television talk show about gay issues. A fundamentalist minister on the panel said, "According to scriptural passages, homosexuality is equivalent to murder or adultery." I recall I had a flash of anger at the hurt directed at my son. When I glanced at Scott and saw that he was unmoved, even amused, my anger turned to relief and even a kind of pity for such a minister. During the audience participation period, which came later, the minister won little sympathy for his cause— a claim that he had a program that could use religious conversion to change homosexuals to heterosexuals. The occasion became a powerful motivating force to become acquainted with what leaders of other religious groups were saying. Through readings I discovered that the message I heard that morning is under challenge by important religious writers from many denominations.

In the past few years, theologians have begun to review the biblical passages that condemn homosexuality as unnatural and sinful. They are realizing that the few condemnatory verses in scripture arose at a time when the authority of the father in the family and the clan was supreme and unquestioned. In those perilous Old Testament times, having children was a major priority for the survival and prosperity of the community. But knowledge of sexuality and procreation was inaccurate. It was thought that each male "seed" was a new being. They assumed that the mother only provided an incubator for the baby. Therefore, any sexual activity that "wasted the seed" was considered a threat to the tribe. Coitus interruptus, male homosexuality, or masturbation were all deemed deserving of a judgment as severe as execution.

The male heads of the families also determined the general attitudes of the clan. While they espoused heterosexuality, they were opposed to the equality of the sexes. The men took multiple wives. Women were viewed as property, valued for their ability to have sons. Female children were sometimes put to death, and women had few rights. Today the majority of people in Western societies consider such beliefs as outrageous violations of human dignity.

As for homosexuality, the old patriarchs scornfully, even cruelly, rejected it, as evidenced by their practice of anal rape against enemies as a way of humiliating them. In this practice, a man was using a man as he would a woman—as an inferior to be dominated. Such practices and beliefs do not fit into our present knowledge of women and homosexual people. Neither do they fit the needs of our society.

But the old ideas die with difficulty, particularly in fundamentalist churches. However, there is new hope, as theologians are now considering the scientific evidence that homosexuality is simply a natural condition for some people in all cultures. More and more of them are maintaining that the religious view of gayness should not be limited by outdated attitudes. A more generous spirit applies the universal biblical messages of loving your neighbor and being fair and nonjudgmental to all persons—gay as well as heterosexual. A better day is breaking for our gay and lesbian children as the new spirit becomes absorbed into religious life.

It is important that parents realize they no longer need to be browbeaten by the Old Testament assumptions. Many religious writers do not condemn either gay people or their parents. Parents who choose to move to full acceptance will find themselves in agreement with the enlightened ideas of many respected religious thinkers.

The issues about religion and homosexuality are complex and emotionally charged. Since many parents have experienced agony about this topic, we feel obligated to face it.

We know that parents will hear about the scriptural passages condemning homosexuality. To ignore these because they are disturbing can leave parents with unfinished emotional business. We think it is better to look the religious issue squarely in the eye.

THE FOUR PREVAILING RELIGIOUS ATTITUDES

We want to illustrate what is going on in religious thought by giving examples of actual arguments now under way.

One of the studies we found most useful was James B. Nelson's *Embodiment: An Approach to Sexuality and Christian Theology*. Nelson, a professor of Christian ethics at the United Theological Seminary of the Twin Cities, identifies what he calls four theological positions toward homosexuality in the contemporary religious scene: (1) a rejecting-punitive attitude (homosexuality should not be accepted and should be punished); (2) a rejecting-nonpunitive attitude (homosexuality is seen as forbidden by scriptures, but homosexual persons should be treated with forgiving grace); (3) a qualified acceptance position (homosexuality is tolerable if it is deemed irreversible and if the relationship is monogamous); and (4) full acceptance (homosexuality should be placed on a par with heterosexuality and the same ethical principles should be applied to both).[2]

I. The Rejecting-Punitive Attitude

Since writing the first edition in the early 1980s, important changes have taken place in the United States. There have been positive gains. A number of communities have included gays in civil rights and hate crimes ordinances. Openly gay congressmen have been elected to the U.S. House of Representatives: Representatives Gerry Studds and Barney Frank (Democrats from Massachusetts) and Representative Steve Gunderson (Republican from Wisconsin). The talk shows repeatedly have had on their programs gays and lesbians and parents from Parents, Families and Friends of Gays (P-FLAG). It has become common knowledge that prominent Republicans have gay family members: Phyllis Schafly's son,

Newt Gingrich's sister, and Barry Goldwater's grandson. A growing number of churches have become "Reconciling" or "Welcoming" congregations. Various polls show that the number of people who have negative attitudes toward gay people has been declining.

But the gains have triggered fear and homophobic reactions among those who have rejecting-punitive attitudes. In the nineties Pat Robertson's Christian Coalition emerged as a major force in this category. The coalition launched well-financed drives in selected states to pass amendments to state constitutions that would deny civil rights to gay people. They have led strong attacks on local school boards whose districts have sex education programs that do not teach that homosexuality is evil, and they have campaigned to fire teachers who acknowledge their gayness—not because they are ineffective teachers but because they are gay. The Christian Coalition has created and distributed videotapes that reinforce all of the negative stereotypes. Reverend Robertson has said that homosexuality seems to be associated with Satanism. He portrays gay American citizens as threats to the moral values of families and communities. Fundamentalist radio stations regularly make virulent attacks on gays and lesbians.

Reverend Pat Robertson's Christian Coalition and other fundamentalists who share his rejecting-punitive attitudes point to passages in the scriptures to justify their arguments.

> So God created man in His own image; in the image of God created He him; male and female created He them. . . . and God said unto them, "Be fruitful and multiply. . . ." (Genesis I: 27–28)

Leviticus 20:13 is one of the Coalition's most frequently quoted passages:

> If a man lie with a male as with a woman, both of them have committed an abomination; they shall be put to death, their blood is upon them.

The fundamentalists do not say why they do not obey the command to kill homosexual people. Others who are told of this passage are more forthright. They carry signs in antigay rallies, "God says, Kill Fags."

While focusing on Leviticus 20:13, they strangely refrain from mentioning other injunctions in Leviticus: "For *everyone* who *curses* his father or his mother *should be put to death*" (Leviticus 20:9); "If a man commits adultery with the wife of his neighbor, both the adulterer and adulteress *shall be put to death*" (Leviticus 20:10). On what grounds do fundamentalists ignore these commands to kill? If they take them literally, there would, of course, be a lot of killing going on.

The biblical literalists also do not explain their decision not to obey passages in Leviticus that prohibit the eating of rabbit, oysters, clams, shrimp, and pork.

James Nelson comments on the selective wrath antigay fundamentalists reserve for homosexual persons:

> Today no major contemporary theologian holds the rejecting-punitive position, and most church bodies in their formal statements have moved away from it. Yet, in practice, it may still be by far the most common orientation throughout the length and breadth of the church in our society. Its theology rests on a selective biblical literalism—selective because other moral issues are not treated with the same kind of moralism at all.[3]

Nelson himself offers some interesting speculations about this selective fixation on homosexuality and the highly charged anxiety and rage that lie behind it. For example, from a Freudian perspective, he points out that even for people whose sex life has been exclusively heterosexual, there may be homosexual feelings present even if relegated to an unconscious level. Freud's idea of reaction formation showed that one way we cope with our own unwanted impulses is by attacking them in others.[4]

Furthermore, the male-dominated tradition contains exaggerated images of masculinity that trigger strong anxiety about homosexuality among men. Homosexuality is viewed as unmanly. It threatens clear masculine gender identity and subverts the ground rules that establish what safe and normal male feelings are supposed to be. Any crossing of the forbidden line unleashes feelings of high danger. As Nelson puts it, "The gay male seems a threat to the importance of super-masculinity, and his very presence seems to call into question so much that many heterosexual men have sacrificed to be 'manly.' "[5] In other words, many gay men refuse to give up the softer, more gentle "feminine" qualities that macho traditions have taught are "only for women." Thus anthropologists have noted the strong tendency of patriarchal cultures to define homosexuality as "the unspeakable sin" while matriarchal cultures have been very different. In the Old Testament there is severe condemnation of male homosexuality while lesbianism is not even mentioned. It is only gay men who suffer the condemnation of the Old Testament. A single passage in Romans 1:26 condemns women "who exchange natural relations for unnatural."

II. The Rejecting-Nonpunitive Attitude

While homosexuality still provokes high levels of anger and anxiety, it is equally true that the Old Testament attitudes are being brought into question.

A first step is the emergence of a rejecting-nonpunitive position. Nelson says this is found among those theologians who reject the harshness of the fundamentalists. They still operate from the assumption that homosexual relations are unnatural in that they violate the commands of the Creator. Karl Barth, a major Protestant theologian, is one who holds this view. But Barth hastens to add that the central theme of the Christian gospel is God's overwhelming grace; therefore, the homosexual person must not be condemned even though homosexuality itself must be. To the theologians, this may seem a generous statement. We who are parents of gay children, however, feel that this position places an unjustified sense of guilt and unworthiness on our sons and daughters.

THE VATICAN'S POLICY FOR ROMAN CATHOLICS   The teaching of Roman Catholic authorities has tended to be rejecting but nonpunitive.[6] In 1975 a statement by the Vatican qualified its traditional condemnation of homosexuality when it stated that the homosexual *inclination* or orientation as an "innate instinct" is not immoral or sinful, but *homosexual acts* are objectively immoral and sinful. Gay people, therefore, must live a celibate life because homosexual behavior violates two fundamental principles of the Church's teaching: (1) sexual (genital) expression of love is intended by God's plan of creation to take place exclusively between a man and a woman in a heterosexual marriage, and (2) genital expression of love is permitted only when "it is open to the possible transmission of new life." (Thus the use of condoms, even in heterosexual marriages, is forbidden.)

In the seventies the Church affirmed the dignity of all persons, condemned homophobic speech or actions, and defended the human and civil rights of gays and lesbians.

The Vatican wavered, however, when it saw a rising acceptance of gay and lesbian persons and the growth of civil rights legislation to protect them against discrimination.

A 1986 letter to the world's bishops from the Vatican Congregation for the Doctrine of the Faith reaffirmed that the homosexual inclination itself is not sinful, but "it is a more or less strong tendency toward an intrinsic moral evil and, therefore, *the inclination itself* must be seen as an *objective disorder.*"[7]

A 1992 Vatican statement qualified its earlier affirmations of civil rights for gays. It argued that the Church and society must oppose any civil rights legislation that appears to condone the homosexual lifestyle because it might undermine the institution of marriage and the family. It argued furthermore that *discrimination* against homosexuals *is not unjust* in such areas as the hiring of teachers or athletic coaches, in the placement of children for adoption or foster care, and in military recruitment. In addition, it argued that discrimination against gay or lesbian persons is warranted when the housing needs of "genuine families" are at stake.

Finally the Vatican Congregation for the Doctrine of the Faith held that when civil rights legislation is proposed to protect behavior "to which no one has any conceivable right, neither the Church nor society at large should be surprised when irrational and violent reactions increase."[8]

We, as parents of gay children, are profoundly disturbed when the Church states that violence against our gay children may be expected when they live with their partners in a way that the Church does not approve of; and when the Church prescribes for homosexuals the same condition of lifelong celibacy that is demanded for men and women who take vows for the holy orders.

III. The Qualified Acceptance Attitude

(1) AN ALTERNATIVE ROMAN CATHOLIC VIEW   As the Vatican, in recent years, has moved in a more restrictive direction, there has been a countermove toward "qualified acceptance" by prominent Catholic theologians, by lay Catholics in the pews, and by members of the clergy.[9]

In the United States, for example, a publication of the Catholic Theological Society of America, *Human Sexuality: New Directions in American Catholic Thought,* holds that homosexual activity can be morally good within the context of a loving, committed relationship.[10] The American bishops stated in 1976 that homosexuals, like everyone else, have a right to respect, friendship, and justice and that they should have an active role in the church.

In 1969 some gay Catholics founded Dignity, an organization to provide pastoral care for Catholic homosexuals whom the Church had neglected. For a while Dignity received support from many bishops. Other grassroots organizations followed: New Ways Ministry, which seeks reconciliation and justice through its educational activities; Communications Ministry, Inc., a support group for gay priests and nuns; and the Conference for Catholic Lesbians. But since the 1986 Vatican letter to the world's bishops, Dignity has been denied use of diocesan facilities by most Church authorities. Many clergy, however, chose to work clandestinely among homosexual Catholics, or used pseudonyms in their writings. Theologians who continued openly to oppose traditional teaching were soon disciplined by the Vatican. For example, John McNeill obeyed an imposed silence for ten years, until he finally chose to speak out, which led to his expulsion from the Jesuits; Anthony Kosnick, senior author of the book *Human Sexuality,* was forbidden to teach sexual ethics; and Charles Curran, perhaps the most prominent moral theologian in America, was removed from his tenured professorship at the Catholic University of America.

As Catholic lesbians and gays feel increasingly marginalized by the Vatican, confusion and anger mount. After receiving support for some years by the Church on civil rights issues, gay Catholics more recently have seen their cardinals in New York, Philadelphia, and Boston become instrumental in defeating proposed gay rights legislation.

As the scourge of AIDS takes a terrible toll across the world, including havoc among heterosexual women and men, more Catholics are deploring the Vatican's policy of strict prohibition of the use of condoms. The Vatican, which champions "The Right to Life," chooses to retain its strictures against contraceptives while tens of thousands of women and men are put in peril.

Finally, as homophobic attitudes seem to increase among Church authorities, they appear to be unable to deal honestly with the disproportionate number of gay clergy and religious in their own ranks.

By the mid-nineties the Church's position on homosexuality was marked by ambiguity and diversity. American bishops are performing a delicate balancing act in attempting to show compassion and care for gay Catholics while trying also to meet Rome's more recent restrictions. Meanwhile, more and more Catholics are resistant to the Church's official pronouncements about sexuality and are asking for full participation in the life of the Church for committed, monogamous gay and lesbian couples.

(2) THE POSITION OF MAINLINE PROTESTANT CHURCHES
Mainline Protestantism has entered its own intense discussions of issues related to homosexual people, and, in general, its denominations assume the rejecting-nonpunitive attitude with some important moves toward greater acceptance. In the eighties and nineties a number of mainline Protestant denominations such as the United Methodist Church, the Presbyterian Church (USA), the Evangelical Lutheran Church of America, the United Church of

Christ, and the Episcopal Church began a process of painful soul-searching and rethinking of their policies toward homosexual people. Two main factors lay behind this development: (1) the decision by growing numbers of gay and lesbian parishioners, ministers, and applicants to seminaries to come out of the closet and tell of the pain they experience by having to conceal the truth about their lives, and (2) mounting evidence from the biological and social sciences that homosexuality is a natural part of the human condition. It has been present throughout history and across human societies. These findings contradict the biblical tradition that homosexuality is a perverse, sinful choice made against the will of God.

Confronting the contradiction has led Protestants to divisive debate in church assemblies. In the mid-nineties the issue remains unresolved. For example, a 1992 General Assembly statement by the Presbyterian Church (USA) acknowledged that the church continues to be in conflict over homosexuality.[11] One faction in the assembly calls for welcoming to membership all people, including those who are openly gay or lesbian; it urges the church to overcome its own homophobia and to work for full civil rights for gay people and for the repeal of laws that discriminate. Other assembly members, more cautious, urge the church to give "definitive guidance" against the ordination of "unrepentant, self-affirming, practicing homosexuals." A 1994 statement acknowledged that the differences between these two points of view "reflect a painful division within our beloved denomination." In 1995, the General Conference of the United Methodist Church voted against a proposal to strike a declaration against homosexuality from the church's Book of Discipline. There remains, however, a deep division in the church over the topic and the debate seems likely to continue in the future. The fear of divisiveness runs across mainline Protestant churches.

Two of the stickiest issues involve the ordination of lesbian or gay ministers and providing commitment or union ceremonies for homosexual couples who have had a long-term, monogamous relationship. In response to the conflicts triggered by such issues a typical response has been to create study commissions. These commissions sometimes work for several years before reporting to general assemblies. The debates that follow often result in forming new commissions for still further study. For example, the 205th General Assembly of the Presbyterians (1993) urged all presbyteries to form study/dialogue groups, which should pay close attention to four factors: (1) the witness of the biblical text; (2) the wisdom of theological discourse; (3) the insights of sociological, psychological, and medical disciplines; and (4) the insights of any who may have been aggrieved by current practices, policies, or laws relating to homosexuality. In 1996, however, the 208th General Assembly voted against ordaining gay and lesbian clergy unless they vowed to remain celibate. This recommendation must be approved by three-quarters of the presbyteries to become part of the church's constitution. As of this writing, the only Protestant denomination to allow the ordination of noncelibate gay men and lesbians is the United Church of Christ.

The differences remain strong even among those who seek guidance primarily from the scriptures. One group points to the five or six passages that condemn homosexuality. Another group points to the teaching of Jesus when he was asked, "Of all the commandments, which is the most important?" His reply:

> The most important is this: Love the Lord your God with all your heart and all your soul and all your mind and strength. The second is, Love your neighbor as yourself. There is no commandment greater than these. (Mark 12: 28–31)

Those who accept this teaching note that there is no reference to homosexuality in the Ten Commandments, and that Jesus chose to say nothing on the subject. What he did say was, "Why do you pass judgment on your brother? Or, why do you despise your brother?" (Romans 14: 10).

In spite of the sharp differences there has been a slow trend toward giving support and affirmation to homosexual parishioners.

The Episcopalians, for example, have passed resolutions that affirm equal rights for gay persons: (1) that gays are children of God and entitled to full civil rights; (2) that ordinances should be passed to protect homosexual spousal rights and benefits; that the same ministerial guidance and support be provided for committed gay couples as is provided for married couples; (3) that Episcopalians direct compassion toward runaway or "throw-away" gay youth and their disproportionate rates of suicide; and (4) that educational materials be prepared for parents who discover they have gay children so that they can accept their children with love.[12]

Once again, however, a minority report said that gays should not be permitted to adopt children, to have spousal benefits, or to have Blessed Union ceremonies.

The Episcopal Church permits individual bishops to make their own decisions regarding ordination of gay or lesbian priests.

In spite of the gradual move toward acceptance the deadlock in the mid-nineties continues. A 1994 statement by a Lutheran study committee finally admitted that no resolution was in sight. In frustration it concluded:

> This church rejects the idea that it must at this time make a definitive legislative decision concerning its teaching on and practice with gay and lesbian persons. Any such decisions would be divisive for this church, and would not be made on the basis of the careful study the topic requires and that should characterize the decisions of the church.[13]

(3) EMERGING VIEWS IN THE JEWISH COMMUNITY   In the American Jewish community the range of attitudes roughly parallels the attitudes found in Christian denominations. On the continuum between rejection and acceptance, Orthodox Jews remain at the rejecting (sometimes punitive) end; the Conservatives have been moving from the rejecting-nonpunitive attitude toward qualified acceptance; while the Reformed community is moving from qualified acceptance toward full acceptance. As among Christians, the trend toward more acceptance among Jewish groups has taken place during the last twenty-five years particularly among Conservative and Reform Jews.

This trend is rooted partly in a renewed remembrance that homosexual people were also sent into Nazi concentration camps; and in changing views of the scriptural tradition. For example, a 1994 policy statement by the Reformed Union of American Hebrew Congregations opened with: "God calls upon us to love our neighbors as ourselves. The prophet Isaiah charges us further: 'Let my house be called a house of prayer for all people. . . .' (Isaiah 56:7)—We Jews are asked to create a society based on righteousness, the goal being *tikkun olam,* the perfection of our world. Each of us, created in God's image, has a unique talent which can contribute to that high moral purpose; and to exclude any Jew from the community of Israel lessens our chances of achieving that goal."[14]

Elsewhere the 1994 statement noted that there are approximately 100,000 gay or lesbian Reform Jews and 500,000 members of the larger Jewish community in the United States. It furthermore stated that "all human beings are created *betselem elohim* ('in the divine image')." The personhood of all must therefore be accorded full divinity. Sexual orientation is irrelevant to the human worth of a person.

While the Conservative movement has not been as accepting as Reform Jews, a 1991 statement by the Rabbinical Assembly acknowledged that "the divine image reflected by every human being must always be cherished and affirmed."[15]

The Rabbinical Assembly also expressed regret that gay and lesbian Jews and their families experience constant homophobic rejection and the fear of violence, and, in addition, feel a painful alienation from their religious congregations.

Thus Conservative and Reform Jews, in their policy statements, hold that the human dignity of homosexual persons should be respected. They should be welcomed into participation in the life of congregations and into the life of youth groups, camps, and schools. Both reaffirm the Jewish ideal of heterosexual marriage. Both acknowledge that the task of reframing policies for homosexuals is complicated by the fact that the Jewish tradition through the ages has condemned homosexual behavior, *and* by the fact that there is less than complete unanimity in the scientific community about understanding homosexuality.

They differ, however, on the particulars of some of the thorniest issues such as: willingness to conduct commitment ceremonies, the admission of gay Jews into rabbinical or cantorial schools, and acceptance of gay rabbis to be congregational leaders.

The Committee on Jewish Law and Standards of the Conservative Rabbinical Assembly in 1991 clarified its policies toward gays by affirming that "(a) We will not perform commitment ceremonies, (b) We will not admit avowed homosexuals to our cantorial or rabbinical schools or to the Rabbinical Assembly or the Cantors' Assembly. At the same time, we will not instigate witch hunts against those who are already members or students."[16]

But the Committee permitted rabbis (who are authorized to make halakic decisions) to decide whether homosexuals will be accepted as teachers or youth leaders. They also gave rabbis the authority, in consultation with lay leaders, to decide whether homosexuals are eligible for honors within worship and for lay leadership positions.

The Conference of Reformed Rabbis, in the early nineties, accepted a Report of the Committee on Homosexuality. Its recommendations were based on in-depth, prolonged study, which included investigation of the research on the origin and nature of sexual identity and testimony from gay and lesbian rabbis and rabbinic students.[17]

The Report affirmed that the majority of Reformed Jews strongly support civil rights for lesbians and gays. It acknowledged that there are gay and lesbian rabbis, usually closeted, who serve their communities with compassion and integrity; but because of the unique position of rabbis as spiritual leaders, the hiring of gay rabbis is sometimes a highly emotional and divisive issue. One of the most controversial issues has been the question of whether gay or lesbian applicants should be accepted by the College Institute for rabbinical training. The report recommended continuation of the Institute's policy that the sexual orientation of candidates should be considered only in the context of their overall qualification and suitability for rabbinical service to Reform congregations. The Conference agreed to admit to the Reformed Rabbinate all graduates of the College Institute, including gays and lesbians.

Reform rabbis have taken no official position on the matter of commitment ceremonies, but individual rabbis do in fact conduct them.

They also acknowledge the existence of homophobic attitudes in congregations and urge development of educational programs in synagogues and in the wider community to promote understanding and respect for lesbians and gay persons. The goal is to make the Union of American Hebrew Congregations "a place where loneliness, suffering and exile end, where gay and lesbian Jews can know that they are accepted on terms of visibility, not invisibility."

Beyond these policy statements Reformed Jews have been active in the political arena. They have, for example, urged governmental units to adopt legislation that will afford spousal benefits to gay and lesbian partners who are in committed relationships, and that governments should pass no ordinances that judge homosexual partners to be unfit to raise children.

Reformed Jews have been in the forefront of opposition to the antigay efforts of the Christian Coalition to create "constitutionally protected discriminatory rights, without limitation, against gay and lesbian people." Such efforts to deny fundamental human rights to homosexual people is viewed as a direct violation of the Jewish faith that justice should be accorded to all of God's children. They call for a boycott by Jews of any state that passes antigay legislation. They warn that the Christian Right is fanning homophobic attitudes in the United States to promote its fundraising efforts and its stealth attacks on public education; and they urge Jews to join other Americans in resisting the regressive agenda of the powerful Radical Right.

IV. The Full-Acceptance Attitude

Beyond qualified acceptance there are important moralists and theologians who embrace full acceptance.

For example, there is the statement by the English Society of

Friends in its widely read *Towards a Quaker View of Sex* (1963): "One should no more deplore homosexuality than left-handedness. . . . Homosexual affection can be as selfless as heterosexual affection and, therefore, we cannot see that it is in some ways morally worse."[18]

Norman Pittenger, a noted Anglican theologian, in *Time for Consent: A Christian's Approach to Homosexuality* further spells out the full acceptance point of view.[19] He says that at base our sexuality means the possibility of expressing and sharing a total personal relationship in love. Gay persons need deep and lasting relationships just as do heterosexuals. Appropriate genital expression should not be denied to either. Pittenger argues that a Christian position should be developed in terms of a central ethical question: "What sexual behavior will serve to enhance, rather than inhibit and damage, the full realization of our divinely intended humanity?" The answer is sexual behavior consistent with an ethic of love—a responsible, ongoing communion with another human that involves commitment, trust, tenderness, and respect. A Christian ethic of love rules out selfish exploitation, cruelty, impersonal sex, obsession with sex, and actions done without mutual willingness. Such an ethic is equally appropriate for heterosexuals and homosexuals; therefore, there should be no double standards.

In *Homosexual Catholics: A New Primer for Discussion,* the authors, in dissent from the Vatican, make a case for full acceptance. According to this position, the norm or ideal in any relationship, regardless of gender, is justice and love. The quality of the relationship, therefore, rather than sex per se determines morality. As the authors of *Homosexual Catholics* put it,

> Since homosexuality has been evidenced at all times and places in human history and in all known cultures to some degree, it could be interpreted as part of the divine plan. While scripture condemns homosexual activity related to lust, idol worship, rape, inhospitality, it cannot be said to condemn loving homosexual relationships between true

homosexual persons. The Genesis account must be seen in light of patriarchal culture, male domination, and propagation of the Jewish race.[20]

THE FULL-ACCEPTANCE POLICY OF UNITARIAN UNIVERSALISTS

The Unitarian Universalist denomination (whose members informally refer to themselves as UUs) in the early seventies began to take seriously its guiding principle "to affirm and promote the inherent worth and dignity of every person." It progressively took a series of steps that have moved it further than any other North American faith tradition toward fully welcoming and affirming gay, lesbian, and bisexual persons.

Following are some examples of stages on the journey:

- In 1974 the UU General Assembly voted to fund an Office of Lesbian and Gay Concerns.
- A resolution in 1980 urged Unitarian Universalist churches to call to the ministry openly gay and lesbian ministers.
- In 1986 the Assembly urged UUs to work to end AIDS discrimination.
- In 1989 it voted to adopt the Welcoming Congregation Program to combat homophobia in congregations and to educate individuals. A *Handbook* was developed to help congregations implement the Welcoming Congregation Program.[21]

The goal was to move to a future where UU churches would follow five principles in becoming truly welcoming places for all persons:

- Be inclusive and expressive of the concerns of gay, lesbian, and bisexual persons at every level of congregational life.
- Celebrate the lives of all people and welcome same-gender couples, recognizing their committed relationships and equally affirming displays of caring and affection with regard to sexual orientation.
- Seek to nurture ongoing dialogue between gay, lesbian,

bisexual, and heterosexual persons, and create deeper trust and sharing.
- Advocate for gay, lesbian, and bisexual people. Attend to legislative developments and work to promote justice, freedom, and equality in the larger society.
- Speak out when the rights of lesbian, gay, and bisexual people are at stake.

By the spring of 1995 sixty-six UU churches had become certified as Welcoming Congregations, and many more are engaging in steps that lead to certification.

In addition to such policy developments within the denomination, UUs began to participate in the public arena for gay rights: In 1993 the Assembly voted to support the wish of gay and lesbian persons to participate in the armed services of their country. It noted that in the past, gay service people had won a wide variety of medals for bravery under fire. In that same year a UU delegation took part in the national march for gay rights in Washington, D.C. In 1994 Unitarians strongly opposed the effort of Pat Robertson's Christian Coalition to add antigay amendments to state constitutions. *The UU World,* the journal of the UU Association, devoted the July–August 1994 issue to a discussion of homosexuality and the denomination. It carried on its cover a quotation from Barry Goldwater, "The Constitution says that *all men* are created equal. It doesn't say that all men are created equal except gays."

Thus the Unitarian Universalist denomination at the national level has adopted the full acceptance attitude, but some individual ministers and congregations still resist open discussion of issues concerning homosexual people.

In general, religious denominations have great difficulty in moving toward full acceptance. The biblical tradition continues to be a major stumbling block. It is relevant to note, however, that homosexuality is not the only issue that has been seriously rethought in modern times. How many people, for example, find their religious leaders demanding that they follow literally the following passages:

Let all who are under the yoke of slavery regard their masters as worthy of all honor. (I Timothy 6:1)

The women should keep silence in the churches. If there
is anything they should desire to know, let them ask their
husbands at home. For it is shameful for a woman to speak
in church. (I Corinthians 14:34–35)

Episcopal Bishop John Spong, in his book *Living in Sin? A Bishop
Rethinks Homosexuality*, faced directly the issue of the Bible and
homosexuality: "If new knowledge about the cause and meaning
of homosexuality confronts us, then we must relinquish our prejudice and the prejudice of Holy Scripture and turn our attention
to loving our gay and lesbian brothers and sisters, supporting
them, and relating to them as a part of God's good creation."[22]
We end this account of the full-acceptance line of thought
among American religious thinkers with a statement by Bishop
Melvin Wheatley of the United Methodist Church:

> I am an enthusiastically heterosexual male. Is my hetero-
> sexuality a virtue? A sign of righteousness? Either an ac-
> complishment or a victory of some kind on my part? Of
> course not. I had nothing whatsoever to do with my being
> heterosexual. It is a mysterious gift of God's grace com-
> municated through an exceedingly complex set of chem-
> ical, biological, chromosomal, hormonal, environmental,
> developmental factors—totally outside of my control. My
> heterosexuality is a gift—neither a virtue nor a sin.
>
> What I do with my heterosexuality, however, is my per-
> sonal, moral, and spiritual responsibility. My behavior as
> a heterosexual may, therefore, be very sinful—brutal, ex-
> ploitative, selfish, promiscuous, superficial. My behavior as
> a heterosexual, on the other hand, may be beautiful—ten-
> der, considerate, loyal, other-centered, profound.
>
> Precisely the same distinction between being a hetero-
> sexual and behaving as a heterosexual applies to homo-
> sexual persons, unless you and I are to be guilty of that
> lowest blow of all, and that is to work by double standards.

Homosexuality, quite like heterosexuality, is neither a virtue nor an accomplishment. It is a mysterious gift of God's grace communicated through an exceedingly complex set of chemical, biological, chromosomal, hormonal, environmental, developmental factors—totally outside of my homosexual friend's control. His or her homosexuality is a gift—neither a sin nor a virtue. What one does with one's homosexuality, however, is one's personal, moral, and spiritual responsibility.

Behavior as a homosexual may, therefore, be very sinful—brutal, exploitative, selfish, promiscuous, superficial. Behavior as a homosexual, on the other hand, may be beautiful—tender, considerate, loyal, other-centered, profound.

With this interpretation of the mystery that must be attributed to sexual orientation, both heterosexual and homosexual, I clearly do not believe that homosexuality is a sin.[23]

PARENTS TAKING A STAND

Ultimately, parents have to work out their personal resolutions. It can be confusing to know what to do in a time of such great cultural change. Eventually, a stand must be taken. We have sympathetic appreciation for parents who struggle toward full and loving acceptance. We believe the following quotations illustrate that parents who move toward acceptance are furthering their own peace of mind and deep personal growth.

My son, Chuck, had given serious thought to becoming a minister. I was an officer in the church and was pledged to uphold the laws and regulations of the church. But when Chuck's situation came into my awareness, things began to seem very hypocritical to me. I felt a lot of resentment toward the church, realizing that he could never be ordained as a minister in that denomination.

About that time I became interested in another denomination which had a different and more generous outlook. As I thought more about it, I decided that I really didn't want to be part of an organization that made such distinctions. So I left the church, which was rather traumatic. Everybody in my family, including myself, had been very active in our old church, so to pull out, you know, did cause a few ripples. But I don't regret it at all. I'm very happy in my present situation.

■

This friend could tell me where anything was in the Bible that I wanted to know. I asked her where did the Bible talk about homosexuality. She told me, and I showed it to Robin, my daughter. "You know," I said, "the Bible says it is wrong." At least I interpreted it to mean that homosexuality is wrong. There was no question in my mind. It bothered me a lot.

But Robin said, "There are so many things in the Bible that are totally obsolete and no longer apply today—like the attitude toward women. Those things are the outdated remnants of an ancient society. The fundamentalists and the moral majority don't abide by those things either. They shrug them off and just say, 'Oh well, those don't count.' Another thing the Bible absolutely forbids is masturbation. Now the sex experts tell us that ninety-nine percent of males and a very high percentage of females have masturbated. It's no big deal: it's normal and healthy. So again, the Bible's rules are shrugged off as obsolete, due to better, more realistic information."

■

You might say that if God accepts people as they are, then we need to accept people as they are. If we condemn people in the name of religion, then we're assuming God's responsibilities. If God is the judge, then let God do the judging.

So I think that the worst thing we can do is to be narrow-mindedly judgmental. Being judgmental about people and their sexual behavior is not a very religious thing to do. I think most of us have all we can do to manage our own lives, let alone make decisions about how other people ought to manage theirs.

Judging people and feeling superior may be more sinful than anyone's so-called sexual misbehavior. How do we know what's in other people's minds and hearts when it comes to sexual practices that are between consenting and loving adults?

■

I know that, because of their religious orientation, many parents feel strongly that gayness is wrong. What can they do?

For one thing, they should do some reading other than materials from their own denomination. Read other religious philosophers who really bring together the teachings of the great religious masters of all times. For example, think of the teachings of Jesus Himself. Over and over again, He preached that the Kingdom of God is within. I see this as meaning that we have an inner teacher. The inner teacher is always saying, "Go into the secret place," which means the inner place where God is within us. We can reach that inner teacher through meditation and prayer, quiet and peace.

I really believe we can get answers from within ourselves, because this inner teacher is our own best self and our own true center.

LEARNING FROM OUR RELIGIOUS DIFFERENCES

In the parents' group we had to confront the diverse religious backgrounds of our members. Among our members there were Roman Catholics, Jews, people from various Protestant denominations, Unitarians, Ethical Culturists, and freethinkers. Our ability to handle this religious diversity was a fundamental challenge and test of our own basic values.

We worked together to find ways that honored the right of each person to hold the religious convictions that fit his or her needs. Some of our most productive activities came from communication with gay support groups in denominations that are beginning to serve their lesbian and gay members. We opened ourselves to learning by handling our religious diversity constructively.

There seems to be a connection between acceptance of sexual diversity and acceptance of religious diversity. As parents of gay people, we are suggesting that Americans can accept diverse forms of sexual expression (always following the principle that freedom of choice bars any form of harm to others) just as Americans permit freedom of religious choice. By asking the American people to accept the hitherto-rejected gay segment of society, we are simply asking that one of the hallowed American traditions be extended to gay people: the tradition of *E pluribus unum* (out of many, one).

Americans developed that principle to make it possible for the diverse groups who came here in search of freedom of conscience to live together peacefully. The underlying social gamble was that tolerance and acceptance could lead to mutual enrichment. It is a principle that has always required stern discipline, embracing, as it does, the right to differ tempered by willingness to give respectful tolerance to dissenting opinions and ways of living.

We think that respect for the American principle of pluralism should be extended to the diverse sexual orientations that are a part of American reality, and that are a part of human reality. As folk singer Holly Near put it, ". . . once felt, if only for a moment, we know the taste of what could be—people sharing a world enriched by their differences, and no one being asked to give up the best of who they are."[24]

If we risk listening carefully to those who seek to combine their gay nature with their deep religious convictions, we might find it a fresh source of spiritual growth. We end with a statement by a young gay man from Dignity, an organization of Catholic gay people with whom our P-FLAG cooperates. He shares the anguish of a personal question: How, in the name of religion, can he be asked to deny one of the deepest truths of his nature—his homosexuality?

He works toward a resolution by contemplating a statement from Mahatma Gandhi: "Inside each of us God has written His clearest messages."

> *Gandhi was one of those remarkable people appearing from time to time on our planet, whose teachings and lives have a profound impact. Gandhi said, "There is no other God than truth. I wor-*

ship God as truth only."And "To me, in its largest sense, religion means self-realization or knowledge of self."

Those of us who are gay should be able to appreciate what Gandhi was saying. Despite the conviction of many religious leaders that they know the truth about homosexuality, we who are gay know that their easy answers just do not make sense to our reality.

How many of these religious leaders with the "answers" know even the most fundamental facts about homosexuality? How many of them have really listened to our stories?

The particular interpretation these people give to certain Bible passages conflicts with the nature God has given us. It is the God of the Bible who has created us with the gift of loving others of the same gender in an emotional, spiritual, and sexual way. Many of us, in order to survive as sane humans, have had to ultimately reject the condemnatory statements of leaders who act as though they are wiser than Gandhi, Jesus, or the Buddha.

To find answers, to come close to the truth, we have to practice the kind of religion Gandhi practices. We have to look into ourselves, into our nature. It is inside each of us that God has written the clearest messages.

If we are seeking the truth, we also know that it is not easy seeing beyond the homophobia inside us. We have to seek, to look within, if we want to follow the path of Jesus, the Buddha, and Gandhi. They were not wedded to doctrines and dogmas, but to the pursuit of truth.[25]

NOTES FOR CHAPTER FOUR

1. Letha Dawson Scanzoni, "Putting a Face on Homosexuality," *The Other Side,* issue 149 (February 1984), pp. 9–10. Reprinted with permission from *The Other Side* magazine, 300 W. Apsley Street, Philadelphia, Pa. 19144.

2. James B. Nelson, *Embodiment: An Approach to Sexuality and Christian Theology* (New York: Pilgrim Press, 1978).

3. Ibid., p. 189.

4. Ibid., p. 202.

5. Ibid., p. 204.

6. The comments that follow are based primarily on an article by Cardinal George Basil Hume, "Note on Church Teaching Concerning Homosexual People," *Origins: CNS Documentary Service*, vol. 24, no. 5 (April 27, 1995), pp. 766–69.

7. Ibid., p. 767.

8. Ibid., p. 768.

9. We are indebted to Jeannine Gramick, S.S.N.D., of New Ways Ministry for the material that follows: *Homosexuality and Catholicism* (unpublished ms.) and "U.S. Catholicism and Homosexuality" (prepared for publication in a *Concise Encyclopedia of Homosexuality*).

10. Committee on the Study of Homosexuality, *Human Sexuality: New Directions in American Catholic Thought*. A study commissioned by the Catholic Theological Society of North America (London: Search Press, 1977).

11. A communication from the General Assembly, Nov. 4, 1992, to Colleagues in Ministry (unpublished).

12. Statement on "Human Sexuality," General Convention of the Episcopal Church, 1994 (B-012a), p. 27; and Statement on "Gays and Lesbians," General Convention, 1994 (C-019s), pp. 62–63.

13. Human Sexuality: Working Draft: A Possible Statement of the Evangelical Lutheran Church of America, October 1994, p. 22 (unpublished).

14. We are indebted to Rabbi Stephen H. Pinsky of Saint Louis, Missouri, for providing us with a policy statement of the Union of Hebrew Congregations, the congregational body of Reform Judaism: "Human Rights of Homosexuals," June 28, 1994 (unpublished).

15. Resolution on "Gay and Lesbian Jews" of the United Synagogue of Conservative Judaism, November 1991.

16. The Committee on Jewish Law and Standards, The Rabbinical Assembly, March 25, 1991. We are indebted to Rabbi Michael Unger of Congregation B'nai Amooni, Saint Louis, Missouri, for providing us with these policy statements.

17. Report of the Ad Hoc Committee on Homosexuality and the Rabbinate, Central Conference of American Rabbis (Reform), June 25, 1990.

18. *Towards a Quaker View of Sex: An Essay by a Group of Friends* (London: Friends House, 1963), pp. 26, 41.

19. Norman Pittenger, *Time for Consent: A Christian's Approach to Homosexuality* (London: SCM Press, Ltd., 1976). See especially Chapter 3, "What Is Man?"; Chapter 11, "An Ethics for Homosexuals"; and Chapter 12, "A Religious Episode."

20. Robert Nugent, Jeannine Gramick and Thomas Oddo, *Homosexual Catholics: A New Primer for Discussion* (Washington, D.C.: Dignity, Inc., 1980), p. 3.

21. Scott W. Alexander, editor, *The Welcoming Congregation* (Boston: The Unitarian Universalist Association, 1990). Also by Scott W. Alexander, a pamphlet, "Unitarian Universalism: A Welcoming Place for Gay, Lesbian, and Bisexual People."

22. John S. Spong, *Living in Sin? A Bishop Rethinks Homosexuality* (San Francisco: Harper and Row, 1988), p. 16.

23. From an address by Bishop Melvin Wheatley (ret.) with his permission.

24. Quote by Holly Near from liner notes written for the song "Unity" on *Journeys* (RR405). Redwood Records. Used with permission.

25. Kevin O'Shea, *Dignity Newsletter*, 3, no. 3 (April 1, 1983).

FIVE

CHANGING
INNER
PERCEPTIONS

I *would like to get to the point where*
I can feel that her homosexuality is as natural for her as heterosexuality is
for me. I'd like to get to the point where homosexuality isn't all that im-
portant in our life with Mary. It won't be easy to do, and I don't know if
it'll come to that. But I hope so.

■

People ask me, "Does it bother you that your son has chosen that kind
of life?" He's no masochist. He'd never "choose" it. It's a hard world out
there. It's hard for everyone, and it's extremely hard for gays and lesbians.
The gay lifestyle involves a lot more responsibility and hazards than the

heterosexual lifestyle. Don did not choose to be gay, but he did choose to live as a gay man with pride.

■

Pat never really blossomed until after she came out about her homosexuality. Her total personality wasn't evident until she knew we had accepted her for what she was. After that she could relax and be herself around us. That was a joy for us to receive.

■

It's sad for me to see the pain, the unhappiness, the degradation, the shunning that our gay children have to go through just because they have a different lifestyle. I believe—I know—that some day our kids can live in a happier world where they will be judged for their deeds and not their sexual orientation.

When we first came face-to-face with our children's gayness, our antiquated value system generated a distressing conflict. Our inner voices told us that being gay or lesbian was unmentionable, scary, sinful, and sick. These beliefs were as deeply entrenched in us as the automatic way we washed dishes or drove a car.

Up until the moment we found out, we had seen our children as healthy, bright, normal, not in any way like our ideas about gay people. Which outlook was correct? We thought we couldn't give up either perception. But we certainly couldn't reconcile them either. To try to get out of this conflict, we could have turned our backs on the homosexuality of our children. But we would still have remained in irreconcilable conflict. Or we could rethink and change our inner perceptions.

The parents interviewed chose to go through a 180-degree change in their perception of their children's sexual nature. Their inward journey was sometimes discouragingly slow; for most it required enormous effort, and for all it took courage. They started out seeing society as being okay and their child as flawed. They ended up seeing their child as okay, but society as flawed.

Some parents experienced the whole range of negative reactions that we will report on in this chapter. Others traveled through only a few. Each had a different time schedule. The personality, personal experiences, and background of each person created a unique reaction within the growing process. No parent traveled through easily. There were many setbacks for each parent as the new learning process gradually became more and more of a comfortable response.

Feelings were the key to opening up the inner world. It was important for parents to acknowledge the depth of whatever negative feelings they had. When these were faced and gradually dropped, they made room for new perceptions that fit their children.

While honesty of feelings is important for adjustment, parents should avoid venting unrestrained frustrations on their gay children. A good friend serves this purpose far better.

Parents who tried to change without going through the work of facing all their negative feelings were disappointed. Such feelings cannot be willed away by good intentions. A few people, very shocked at negative feelings toward their own children, sugarcoated them. When we heard parents say they had no problems with their children's gayness, we wondered if they might be denying very real problems. Such denial could lead to a stagnation of grief.

We are sure that gay and lesbian children are often disappointed with the negative reaction that their parents first show. But early reactions are not a reliable indication of whether parents will move toward and beyond acceptance. A much better indicator is a willingness to open themselves to new information and to maintain contact with their child.

OPENING UP TO FEELINGS

In recalling their early feelings and experiences, many of the parents we interviewed told us that for days and sometimes weeks after learning of their child's gayness, they were consumed with the news. Homosexuality filled the mind and was the thought for the day. For most there was a sense of tragedy, of loss, and, for a time, an all-consuming pain. The very foundation on which their daily lives was built felt shaky and insecure.

After reading the letter that Mary wrote telling us she was gay, I couldn't think of anything else. I went about my daily work, but the thought of Mary's being gay was never out of my mind for an instant. I had difficulty sleeping at night, and the very second that I would wake, the thought would be with me. Over and over I kept thinking, "What are we going to do?"

■

The word homosexual seemed planted across my forehead for days after Matt told us he was gay. It was the first thing I thought about in the morning and the last thing I thought about at night. I even dreamed about it.

Grief

These early feelings and actions were usually a part of an encompassing grief. Many parents were surprised at the intensity and length of time it took to grieve. One mother compared her grief to that of parents whose child has died. Isolation and a lack of help magnified their sense of desolation.

I was devastated. I can't even describe my feelings. I was just so numb for a while.

■

Sometimes I even thought it would have been easier if my daughter were dead. I didn't think this very long or very often, but it does show how upset I was.

■

One of the most painful parts was facing the issue of a perfect family. It was very important to my self-esteem that I see myself as a VERY GOOD MOTHER with capital letters. And VERY GOOD MOTHERS raise per-

fect children. For a while a gay son was far from being my idea of a perfect child.

■

I thought, "I'll never have grandchildren from James. James will never bring home a lovely girl and say, 'Well, this is the one, Mom.'"

There was a certain amount of grief for a while—grief that my dreams were shattered. I didn't have them written down, but they were there, somewhere in the back of my mind, and they had been killed.

Anger

Anger was not uncommon for parents. It struck in various ways. Sometimes it was directed at the child. Many times the son's or daughter's lover got the brunt of it. At times anger was veiled, but often it was direct, and parents said and did things they later regretted. This early anger masked their frustration, fear, and hurt. It signaled to parents that they had a lot of work to do. They sensed that something was drastically amiss, but at this level they often did not understand exactly what that was.

I was filled with both anger at being told and gratitude that she had not told us earlier. Then I would get angry that she hadn't trusted us enough to tell us. My thinking and feelings made no sense at all.

I didn't stop to think of her pain. I thought of myself more than I did of Sarah. It was all too new for me. We were getting ready for the wedding of our son, Joe, at the time that Sarah chose to let us know she was gay. I thought she used poor timing, and I was angry at her for that. I wondered why she picked that particular time to tell us, and I thought it was terribly unkind of her.

We had some pretty harsh words over the phone several times. I think Sarah expected too much too soon. One statement Sarah made was "I want you to be as happy for Sheryl and me as you are for Joe finding someone to love." Mark and I almost simultaneously blurted out, "How can we be happy about that? Find a man to love. Then we'll be happy." That was a very cruel thing. I can't speak for my husband, but I was trying to hurt her as she had hurt me. It's nothing to be proud of, a revelation like that, but it's the truth. After that there was no communication for some time.

■

My son had a friend who told him how his parents reacted when they found out they had a gay son. That boy's mother said to him, "You got that at school. I didn't bring you up to be that way. You just leave that right where you got it." She said it over and over to him.

And his father would say, "God made Adam and Eve. He didn't make Adam and Steve."

■

After all this time I still hate John's first lover with a passion. I could still punch him if I had the chance. It wasn't his fault, but I hated that S.O.B.

Sadness

For a while most parents were sad and depressed. Tears were frequent. For some, day-to-day activities became difficult to perform.

I just went to pieces—inside, not outside—because Tom still didn't know. I thought, "I can't go to work." Then I'd think, "I have to go to work. The bills are going to accumulate whether Jerry's gay or not. The world is going to go on too."

■

Mark and I did not know how to handle it. We didn't know where we were going to go with it. We didn't know how to act. I was hurt and confused. I wondered what I had done to deserve this.

■

It's been six months now, and I still find myself crying. At first I cried all the time. I'd be at work and all at once I'd tear up. I wondered if I would ever get over that sad feeling.

■

It hurt so bad there were times when I was sorry I had to wake up and face the day. I often wished I could die.

■

I have periods when I accept this very nicely. Other times I sink into depression. Then I find I just have to get away from thinking about Marilyn's being gay. I don't want to think or talk about it. But sometimes I feel I just have to talk. Right now, for instance, I'm finding that talking is good.

Loneliness

At first most parents thought their families were the only ones who had a gay child. Some felt lonely and had trouble relating to old friends. Even the most common social interactions became uncomfortable.

I felt so alone. I cried, and I didn't know why. I thought, "How am I going to live through this?" I'm a single parent and didn't know where to turn.

■

It was really hard for us to enjoy any kind of social contact with people for a while. We got so tired of hearing people ask if Tony had a steady girlfriend. Those kinds of questions were hard. So we withdrew inside ourselves.

Guilt

Guilt implies that something is wrong, and that someone must be made to take the blame. Parents of lesbians or gays in our society are often made to feel like criminals, and frequently they are all too willing to assume a criminal status. Many parents interviewed also felt guilty and searched for a culprit to share their presumed failing. They blamed their child, the child's lover, someone in the child's past, or the other parent. Guilt and blame are a natural part of any loss. But such reactions, if continued too long, can trap parents in a self-destructive pattern.

It just stands to reason that mothers are usually closer to their sons in the early years than fathers are. Now they have found out that gay men have no more problems because of this than nongay ones. That whole idea was wrong. But I suffered a lot of guilt. I thought that the family was the cause of homosexuality and that the mother was a big part of that cause. I was quick to condemn myself. You know, everyone has an opinion about homosexuality, but nobody really knows. There are a lot of hurtful ideas going around.

Now I don't see our family as different from other families. The troubles that we had, even though they were painful, were the usual troubles that many families have.

■

Even now when I think of how Greg was when he was a little boy, I feel guilty. I wish I could have helped him more. I wish I could have been more accepting.

■

I was plagued with feelings of guilt like "Were we a bad family? Were we bad parents? Was I a bad mother?"

Failure

For many, producing children who did not fit easily into society also produced a loss of their feelings of competence as men and women. For a while some parents were left with a feeling of failure that was intense.

When I was younger, I felt okay about myself. But after Roy told us he was gay, for a while I thought I was a failure as a man.

■

My mother was a drug addict and she abused me. But I thought she was a better mother than I was because she didn't raise a gay child.

Shame

Feelings of shame engulfed many of the interviewed parents as they began to deal with the taboo that accompanies homosexuality in this society. They were often unaware of how strong this taboo was until they were faced with it in their own family.

There was an added problem. Parents were usually in their forties and fifties before being confronted with society's prejudice
against their children. Settled into a way of life, they were confi-
dent that they knew how to act in this complicated world. Suddenly
they felt they were members of a minority group being openly attacked, and they had not developed the defenses to cope with this
onslaught.

*I worried about what people would say. Would they laugh? Would they
look down on us? We didn't tell anybody for quite a while.*

■

*It sounds ridiculous to be so concerned about what people think. Why
should that worry anybody that much? But it does. It seems to intimidate
a lot of parents, and it certainly intimidated me. I thought, "What if
people gasped! What if they whispered behind my back! What if! What if!
What if!"*

■

*There weren't many books in the library about homosexuality, and I
couldn't even go get them if they were there. I wondered how I could check
out such books without looking like I had a gay son.*

■

*For the first time in my life I was ashamed of one of my children. I had
always thought my kids were better than other kids that I knew. My feeling
of superiority quickly vanished.*

Fears of Catastrophe

Sometimes parents were filled with overwhelming and frightening
thoughts. They imagined catastrophic happenings or pictured
their children as being abnormal.

*There is an in-law in the family who is so far to the right that he is en-
tirely capable of going to the bar association and reporting her. Her career
could be ruined.*

■

I knew she was going to be a schoolteacher. I also knew what people think about a homosexual teaching school. I knew what society thinks about gays, period. I thought, "She's going to have a miserable life."

■

For a while I even thought of my son as a pervert.

Questions About Their Own Sexuality

The homophobia that most parents started out with often caused them to doubt their own heterosexuality, the quality of their role modeling, and/or the quality of their genes. Often there was a fear of having "opposite-gender" traits. They examined their behavior in detail and worried that anything other than total societal conformity might have contributed to their child's being gay. Some even wondered if they themselves were somehow latent homosexuals.

Most parents have picked up mixed messages about what constitutes an ideal parent. We have been caught in a bind by the changing standards for parenting. Since no parent perfectly fulfills the ideals that our society imposes, parents of gays have an almost built-in case for feeling unsure about the example they have set.

Almost any caring mother, single or married, may ask, "Was I too strong? Was I being seductive when I was cuddling my son? Was I castrating when I gave him advice or asked him to help me with the dishes? Did the decisions I had to make somehow make men appear weak?"

A father might ask, "Does enjoying the company of other males make me partially gay? Am I too domestic because I like to cook? Should I have insisted that my daughter wear dresses more often? Was I wrong to let my son drop out of Boy Scouts? Should I have been a 'tough guy' like John Wayne who rarely showed his feelings? If I had been home more, would my child be gay?"

While this was a difficult revelation for them to make, some parents were willing to discuss the doubts that crossed their minds about their own sexual orientation.

I think we all feel love toward members of our own sex, especially if they have any trouble. I often want to hold my friends when they're in sorrow. To love another woman is very natural to me, but to love her sexually is not my norm.

I think anybody who finds out there is someone gay in the family is going to stop and think, "If the situation had been right, would I have been that way?" I started examining my sexual feelings toward other women and realized I'd never looked at any woman and had sexual thoughts. So I didn't see how I could possibly be gay. Jerry knew he was gay when he was in high school; but when I was that age, I wasn't looking at girls. I was looking at boys. These are the kinds of thoughts that probably go through everybody's mind.

When you are faced with the homosexuality of your child, you're faced with something you don't quite understand. I wondered if I could be homosexual too. I have examined and questioned myself on it. Finally I decided that people are really socially conditioned from the time they are little to be heterosexual. But some people just cannot be heterosexual; for them the conditioning just doesn't work.

I was a real tomboy when I was a little girl, and I guess I had more "masculine" traits than some girls. But I've never had any homosexual attraction even in my fantasies. Maybe if I were in prison and there were no other sexual outlets, I might have some sexual interest in women. I can understand in an intellectual way how a lesbian feels, but from a gut level I can't.

For a while there I wondered if homosexuality ran in the family. I have a brother who is gay and a son who is gay. I thought, "Am I sure I'm to-

tally straight?" It very definitely bothered me for a while. Now I've reached the point where I see no reason to question my own sexuality. I don't think it's bad to have a gay son or brother anymore.

MOVING TOWARD ACCEPTANCE

As parents learned to shed their guilt and become more relaxed about their parenting, they became aware of their own inner prejudices and experienced a desire to be rid of them. They realized their daughter or son felt pain too and was like them in her or his needs, wants, and desires. In a way there was a reversal of roles, as parents sought help from their children. From this, most parents developed a new understanding and pride in their child. Homosexuality was put in its proper perspective as being a natural variation of sexuality.

Commitment to Child Renewed

The common denominator among parents was a sense of permanent involvement and commitment to their child. They did not want any separation. Even in the depths of their early grief, there were strong expressions of parental concern and loyalty.

I could never turn my back on any of my children. I don't know what they would have to do for me to throw up my hands and give up on them. My love for Dan was greater than my anxiety about his homosexuality. The best way I can say it is that for me love conquered all. I knew I would stick by him no matter what.

■

At first I figured that we would remain close. He would still be a part of our life, but I wasn't sure if I could be a part of his. I wondered about going to visit him and if we would get to know his friends. It worried me because I didn't want to feel separate from my son in any way. Time has proved this worry to be totally wrong. Harry and I are as close to Eric as we ever were.

Accepting Reality of Child's Gayness

When parents were able to accept the reality of having a gay child, their despondency lifted noticeably. As they turned and faced the reality of their situation, they found it was not as bad as they first feared. The welfare of their child resumed its high priority on their list of concerns.

Once I accepted the fact that Dan was gay, I had a lot of fears about it. Oh, not about how I would handle it, but that he might get hurt. He might have some experience that was detrimental to him mentally or physically or in some other way. I was more worried about his well-being than I was about anything else.

We have accepted Mike's homosexuality. We gave up all those unrealistic dreams. This freed us from false hopes. Mike doesn't have to go through that constant battle between what he is and what we thought he should have been.

Once I got the obstacle of cause out of the way, I started putting the pieces together. My anger left, and our parent-child relationship became comfortable. I didn't feel disappointment that he was gay instead of straight. That he will probably never give me grandchildren doesn't bother me, because that's just the way his life is going to be.

There's a certain amount of relief on my husband's part as well as mine. I don't think his and Robin's relationship has changed much. It might be a little better because my husband is no longer wondering what could be wrong. He now knows why there was a barrier between them.

I remember that one time he said to Robin, "I'm going to take you out and buy you some feminine clothes." So they went shopping, and he spent hundreds of dollars on all these clothes for her. Most of them she has never had on her body. She went along with it just to appease him because she cares so much about him.

Even though I can't change the fact that she's a lesbian, in the back of my mind I still hope she can find some guy. But it's a relief to know about this because I used to wonder why she was not dating much, or why she hardly ever wore dresses. Now I know why things are happening, and the atmosphere is conducive to talking it over.

Confronting Inner Prejudice

Parents have to live with the fact that they rarely questioned and may have participated in prejudicial remarks. It was not at all unusual for parents, as members of this homophobic society, to recall laughing at gay jokes, agreeing with negative comments, and even making such comments themselves.

At the intermission of a performance of Hamlet *I began talking about homosexuality, and of all things, I said to my daughter, "I find homosexuality repulsive. I can't imagine a man loving another man."*

And I'm sure she must have thought, "Oh my God! How will I ever tell Mom if that's the way she feels?"

■

People have to learn. There was a time when I was in a skit that involved the problems of homosexuals, and we laughed because one of the fellows cut up so much. I think back to how I laughed about it. I wouldn't do that now. I wouldn't even think the skit was funny now.

■

I never did like to be in the presence of any homosexuals. When I was young, I avoided them. I showed my distaste. I feel a guilt about that now.

Transition: Subtle Prejudice. As the learning process continues, outward prejudice can be replaced by a subtle prejudice. This change signals that parents are moving away from their early ideas and into a more accepting attitude. In this interim period, parents often think of their child as being handicapped or less than fully normal.

Sometimes without realizing it, I compare my gay child to a child who has a handicap like blindness or deafness.

∎

You could say if I was really accepting I wouldn't care who knew it. Since I still care about some people's knowing, I would say I am not 100 percent accepting. I still sometimes see Jean as a handicapped child. When I realize this about myself, I do feel bad. But I'm having a hard time letting go of the feeling.

Realization: Desire to Change. We found another common thread among parents who adjusted and faced their prejudice. They sensed their child could not change. They knew they were the ones who would have to change.

I don't know how much unhappiness Mary has had. I don't even know if I could bear to know. I can't shield her from the rest of the world, but I can be sure that I don't cause her any future pain.

∎

I felt bad about my feelings. I got to thinking about it, and realized I didn't even know where my ideas came from. I decided I had to do something to wipe away what I thought about her being gay.

Action: Giving Up Guilt. After accepting the reality of gayness in the family and their own prejudice, these parents began to see how their guilt feelings were preventing them from changing themselves. They had to let that guilt move to a back burner in order to get out of the bind.

We have been brainwashed that if we have a child who is different in any way, then the parents are automatically at fault. Parents should not assume any guilt because no crime has been committed. I don't think parents are the cause. I don't see anything wrong with homosexuality anyway.

∎

As parents we have a set of expectations for all our children. Then the children grow up, and somehow they just don't meet all those expectations. They have ideas of their own. I think parents have to come to terms with that. Some of us let go better than others.

Changing the Focus from Parent to Child

Awareness of Child's Pain. Parents have glimpses of the child's pain from the first. But until some healing occurs, they are too preoccupied to empathize deeply with their child's difficulties. As the initial grief eases, the pain their son or daughter experienced comes more and more into the foreground. Some parents have had to face the possibility that their child may have seriously considered suicide.

We know of no parents who died because of finding out they have a gay child. What we do know is that some gay people in our community have chosen to die because of a lack of support. To have a life end because that person is gay or lesbian is an abomination and an irreplaceable loss.

If I knew then what I know now, I would have raised a much healthier son. He would never have felt ashamed—or at least I would have done my utmost to keep him from feeling ashamed. I would have catered more to the things he showed interest and ability in. I would have made him feel proud of his accomplishments.

■

Sometimes I think about all those years when I thought she was heterosexual. It must have been hard for her.

■

This is something Mary has lived with since a very early age. I've heard from a friend of Mary's that she tried desperately, over a long period of time, to change. She was even engaged at one time several years ago. She told me that for a while she figured if society couldn't accept her being gay, she would try marriage. Thank goodness she realized it wouldn't work and broke off the engagement after about six months. I think it was very wise on her part.

There would have been a lot of unhappiness and probably a divorce. He is a fine young man, and Mary knew she would have caused him a good deal of pain. She cared enough for him not to hurt him.

■

I don't want to say I'm overjoyed that my child is gay. I don't think any of us are glad that our children will probably have a difficult time. But it's good to see that my son has found a place for himself; that he is in a world he is comfortable with and where he feels completely at ease. When he was trying to fit into the heterosexual world, he felt he wasn't making it, and was seriously depressed. I was really worried about him. I think sometimes young people commit suicide over this. They feel they have failed to meet their family's and society's standards and that the impulses they have are completely wrong. I see Chris as being satisfied now, and it's a relief for me to see him happy.

■

My daughter told me that when she was in high school, she was so depressed she thought of just walking slowly across a busy street so she'd be killed. This shocked me more than her telling me she was a lesbian. I was really upset about it.

■

In one of our talks Eric indicated that when he had worked at a music camp one summer, he had thought he'd be better off swimming out and drowning himself. Then he thought about it and decided we'd rather have him alive and homosexual than not alive. Learning about this was almost more than I could handle.

I assured him that he was right, and that whatever he was, we'd rather have him alive. Later I kept thinking about what would have happened if we had gotten a call telling us Eric had drowned. I kept telling myself that would have hurt worse, that I really hadn't experienced the worst that could happen. And, you know, that kept me going. At least I still had Eric.

Awareness of Child's Needs and Wants. Once the parents are aware of the pain their child has experienced, they are then free to understand the child's needs, desires, and wants. There is a return to the old familiar and comfortable relationship, but with an added dimension. Parents can step aside and see their son or daughter as a young adult.

In my experience with my son, I see that his biggest hurdle, emotionally, was coming out. Since doing that he seems so in control of himself. He seems in balance.

■

Lately I've come to the conclusion that Mary's feelings for Sheryl are as deep and sincere as mine are for Mark. I don't see how such feelings could be all that wrong. Love is love no matter which way you go.

■

I just want them to be happy. I think people need each other. I don't care what type of relationship it is, everyone needs someone to feel close to.

■

At first I thought being gay was shameful and perverted, but now I think Herb is fascinating. He's going to live a different kind of life. The lifestyle is interesting, and some things about it are admirable. He lives a lot more in today's world than I do. I think my life would be happier if I could do that.

■

She's happy with her situation, and I'm satisfied with that. If I had to watch her suffer, I wouldn't like that at all. Most of us really want our children to be fulfilled and happy.

Accepting the Lover and Displays of Affection

One of the last actions that parents are able to accept is overt physical affection between people of the same sex. It took a lot of peeling away of the homophobic onion skin before parents were able to approve of physical affection between their gay child and his or her lover. They spent hours on family rules concerning this issue. They had difficulty accepting such innocuous actions as hugging, patting, and kissing. Parents worried extensively about sleeping arrangements when gay couples visited.

Gay and lesbian children can help parents with this problem through a gentle educational procedure. It helps for the children to talk to the parents about the sexual nature of gays and lesbians. In many cases, just answering questions as positively as possible is enough. When parents understand the similarities between the sexual lives of gays and nongays, they are better able to accept the differences.

After parents think about and assimilate a concept about the sexuality of their children, they are ready to see open affection. All of this happens in small increments. If children expect too much too soon, they will be disappointed. But most parents, whose children persistently and lovingly refuse to deny their sexual and coupling nature, lose much of their feeling of discomfort in the presence of physical affection.

I have to admit that even now when I see heterosexuals holding hands or kissing in public, I pay less attention to it than I would if they were homosexuals.

■

I feel uncomfortable seeing Jean kiss Cathy. I hope I'll get over this feeling. I know it's unfair, because I don't feel that way when I see straight couples doing the same thing. I try not to feel like this, but it's hard not to.

■

I've never seen any affection between Mary and Sheryl when they're around us. I think that would be difficult for me, the first time anyway. Perhaps after a while I'll be able to handle it better. For now I try not to think of the sexual aspect of their relationship. While it's hard for me to accept, I don't really think it's wrong on their part. I'm sure they're serious in their commitment.

Absorbing Strength from Child

Children can teach parents about gayness in many ways, not the least of which is the example they set. As the parents become the students instead of the teachers, they are comforted by the character and self-assurance of their child.

I have such admiration for Rachel's character and personality, that I knew if she felt this way, it wasn't immoral in her mind. And if it wasn't immoral in her mind, then it wasn't in my mind either.

■

One friend did ask me, "Don't you really wish that he was straight?" and I can very honestly say, "No. I am thrilled that I am even in the same family with this young man."

If he were in great emotional distress because of being gay, then I would certainly see that he had good counseling. But since he isn't, I feel totally at ease about the whole thing. And I feel very strongly that if he does have problems of any kind along the way, they probably won't have anything to do with his homosexuality. His sexuality is not segregated from the rest of him.

Finding Renewed Pride

As inner perception permanently changes, parents spontaneously speak of pride in their gay son or daughter. They are aware of the courage shown by all these daughters and sons who have made a place for themselves in a hostile world.

I think Gary is strong and can handle being gay pretty well. Believe it or not, I also think we gave him that. We gave him a stable home to grow up in, and there wasn't any question but that he was loved. When he came to tell us he was gay, he wasn't really worried that we would kick him out.

■

Don is so knowledgeable. I feel a sense of pride about what he's doing. He's working with the people in Dignity to help gays and lesbians who are Catholic. He's helping to wash away a lot of pain. It's a slow process, but at least it's starting. I think we can say there are clear skies ahead. I don't know if it will happen in our lifetime, or even in Don's lifetime. But— maybe in our grandchildren's lifetime—lesbians and gays will be accepted.

■

Linda has dedication, feelings, and concerns. She fulfills her responsibility, always has. She feels a closeness to the family and corresponds with us. She sends birthday cards, and she telephones, and that sort of thing. She is negotiation chairman for her union and is doing a good job. She has been quoted in the paper. She doesn't jump into things with the brashness of youth, but rather she studies things through very carefully. I am most proud of her.

■

I am proud of how Greg has handled himself. He chose a healthy way to enter the homosexual world. He has selected partners who are supportive. He demands that he be accepted for what he is. He refuses to hide.

Learning to Laugh

Humor is a great healer for parents who are working through their homophobic perceptions. Laughing about a situation causes our catastrophic thoughts to assume less importance and to loosen their hold on us.

Parents are often able to see the ridiculous part of some of their early ideas. One group of parents had a good laugh when they found the only thing they had in common was that they all drove Volkswagens. In the middle of a particularly trying conversation, one of the fathers said, "Sometimes we sound just like a soap opera."

Letting Go

As parents continued their work, they let go of a lot of the old dreams and ideas. They lost that vague sense of being responsible for all their son's or daughter's problems and changes, and chose not to assume guilt. This stage was a good time, a hopeful time, a time of growth for both parent and child.

Before I knew he was gay, he was keeping his distance from me and the rest of the family. But since we've known, everything has been running smoothly. I don't know how his life will evolve, or where he will ultimately choose to live. But I don't think that, because of us, he will choose to live far away.

■

We let each of our children go their own way. We never tried to hold them back. We did the best we could up to a point, and then our lives were ours and their lives were theirs. All of us have hopes for our children, but you can carry that only so far; then they have to go their own way.

■

I think there are disturbed elements in every human being. In every family there are disturbed elements and in every marriage there are disturbed elements. Ours had some of those too.

At first I felt guilty about not being the perfect parent. But I was doing the best I could, and our son has turned out to be a wonderful person. He's a child I'm proud of. He's contributing to the world. He's helping people who are suffering, and he's hurting nobody. His lifestyle is one I think people could learn from, including myself. I feel that his sexual orientation isn't all that much of a disappointment anymore, if it's a disappointment at all.

Getting There: Placing Homosexuality in the Proper Perspective

The hard work has paid off when parents have no questions about what the real problem regarding homosexuality is. They know it is society's pervasive and unreasonable fear about gayness that causes the damage. They long for society to change, and some of them will move toward becoming a force in helping that change take place.

I see her lifestyle as perfectly okay. I still think it's inconvenient in our society. It's unfair that our society penalizes gays and their families. But that surely isn't Kate's fault. I want society to change, not Kate, and I'm working to do just that.

■

You don't have to have a gay child to have problems with your children. There are many things that you go through with them that are traumatic. Having a gay child is just one of the things. I think that outlook has helped me accept Rachel. I try to look at our family—and the things we've been through—as a whole, and I realize that this is just one more of the many things that can happen when you have children.

TAKING THE STEP BEYOND

After examining and reaffirming the relationship with their son or daughter, many parents became realistically aware of what their child would have to face. They began to see their child as part of a larger group that is unfairly treated. Each felt that just as his or her own child deserved civil rights, understanding, and love, so did all gays and lesbians. As their own child deserved to be judged on merit and individual effort, so did all gay persons. Parents realized that gays and lesbians are like themselves with the only difference being in sexual orientation. Many parents committed themselves to the work of eliminating homophobia wherever they found it.

Widening the Focus

With their developing empathy for the feeling of being in a minority position, parents experienced and understood the deep need of lesbians and gays to live with pride. A major connection had been made. No longer could parents view gayness as a lifestyle that was "out there." Instead, it would now be a part of their day-to-day existence.

It dawned on me that Karen had gone through a period of thinking that we'd be better off without her. I began to feel something for those young people whose folks kick them out and won't accept them. I felt anger at the parents, and I felt so much sorrow for the children. You hear these suicide statistics and think, "What kind of parent could do that to a child knowing that it might cause the child to commit suicide?"

■

Sally chose to go with her nature and not fight it. Otherwise, I think she would have continued to be miserable and depressed indefinitely. Why should gay or lesbian people be miserable because they have been told to deny something that doesn't hurt anybody? Many of them have told me that being gay was their nature, and they either go with it or be unhappy. I think it is immoral not to go with your natural sexual tendencies as long as you're responsible.

■

I had an experience that helped me understand the pain of being a member of an "undesirable" minority—it helped me understand what gays go through.

I went to a New Year's Day open house with my son shortly after he had come out to us. Everyone there was gay except Lois and me. I was the only heterosexual male.

For some reason, the gay men were suspicious of me and wouldn't talk to me. There was this invisible barrier between us. They couldn't seem to cross it, and I didn't know how to. It was an eerie feeling. Maybe I unconsciously contributed to the barrier.

It was an enlightening situation. I saw things from the viewpoint of being a minority. It opened my eyes to a lot of things—not just about gay people, but about the feelings of any minority. I got a terrific insight that day.

■

The statistics say that one in ten persons is gay—perhaps even more. As a high school teacher, I know that in every class I have, there is someone who is gay. One of the saddest things is that no one can help them.

I am also aware of the ridicule that young people, who are not sure of their sexual identity, go through. One of the favorite things my high school students do is to accuse one another of being gay. It's just a constant thing. Faggot is the big name they call each other when they're in junior high. There's a lot of that in high school too. I am sensitive to how that makes young people feel when they are in the midst of learning about themselves. It has to be difficult.

Recognizing That Society's View Is the Real Problem

While parents were in the process of shedding their misinformation, there was a gradual unfolding of how unfair this society's view on homosexuality is. After a time they knew without question what the real problem was and is. It is not with homosexuality per se; it is with what happens to gays and lesbians in our society.

How I wish people could realize that just because a person's lifestyle is different, it is not necessarily wrong. What's right for one person can be wrong for another. I think everyone can live with this idea, because I am living with it. Someday, maybe, humanity will not be all that concerned about lifestyles, about the color of a person's skin, or about what God someone worships. We'll just try to live in harmony, letting other people live their life as best they can and find happiness where they can.

■

If homosexuality were taken for granted as much as heterosexuality is, there wouldn't be any problem. A lot of us think of homosexuality only in terms of sexual relations, but it's much more than that. My daughter is happy the way she is, and it is a whole way of life for her.

You know, anything that gays do sexually, heterosexuals also do. Sexual customs have changed in the last few years. It's more liberal now. There's a feeling that anything is acceptable between consenting, heterosexual adults. But when lesbians and gays do the same thing, it is considered shocking, immoral, disgusting, and sinful.

Trying to Do Something About the Problem

Some parents develop a deep desire to fight back. They want to make life better for their own child and for all gays and lesbians. They are willing to take risks.

I don't have much to leave Betty. But I'm going to fight until my last breath to make it better for her. I want to get the laws changed. I want to change the political system. I may not be able to get anything done, but at least I'm going to try.

■

Chris suggested that we consider starting a parents' group. He thought it would be a good, interesting, and satisfying project for us. Jack and I agreed, and we contacted the Metropolitan Community Church. Slowly the group took shape, and we helped other parents.

■

About the time that Amy came out, the crisis hot line needed volunteers. I had just found out that Amy had considered killing herself. Volunteering for the hot line grabbed my attention because I thought, "Maybe I can help someone like Amy."

As it happened, after I completed my training my very first call was from a man who was gay. I think I was really able to help him. I took that call as a sign that I was supposed to do that work for a while. And I did. I talked to many other gay people.

Setbacks

Sometimes when they least expected it, parents would find themselves falling back into old perceptions. It was disturbing, but it was only a temporary setback. What slowly came to consciousness was that they had experienced an inner change as they resolved the issues surrounding the setback. As parents began to investigate the sources of their reversals, they looked inside and saw that they were being controlled by old messages that no longer applied. The frightening thoughts were like holes in their thinking that they had to reweave with new information and new attitudes.

As a result, the entire fabric of their thinking became stronger. A new and surprising sense of freedom emerged. Parents frequently reported feeling more grown up and more in charge of their lives than ever before. They discussed these temporary setbacks in our interviews.

A boyhood friend of Mark's came by to return a tool he had borrowed. He asked me how Mark was doing. I knew he was aware that Mark is gay, but I found myself fumbling for words. After Dave left, I felt like I had let Mark down. And I had.

■

I was feeling pretty good about Jane's being a lesbian when I picked up a pamphlet about lesbians. It said Jane had a choice. That pamphlet was written by someone who should know, and it really shook me. I wondered if Jane wanted to hurt me by choosing to be a lesbian. For a day or so I really thought she hated me and wanted to punish me by being gay. I was in a panic.

Then I talked to another mother who had had something like this happen to her. She told me how hard it was to find good information because few people have really researched why people are gay, but everybody had opinions about it. She said she'd just decided to pay attention to articles and books that made her feel better.

I thought that was a pretty good idea and decided to try it the next time. It took me a few days, but just talking with her had eased my scared and hurt feelings. I wish I knew for sure why Jane is gay, but I'm beginning to wonder if it is all that important after all.

The Light at the End of the Tunnel

Parents know the struggle will never really end because the reality of their lives and their children's lives is forever changing. But they are better prepared to face the future. They have grown to be more mature and less judgmental.

When my daughter was little, there were some things I was very moralistic about. I had some holier-than-thou attitudes. But now, after going through this experience of having a lesbian child, I have become more aware of what is going on. I'm not that judgmental of people anymore.

■

I think we're better people because of it. Our accepting it has helped our son reach his potential. He is not bothered with any aspect of being gay. And we're not either.

■

We have grown up as we examined our inner thoughts. It's almost indecent how much fun this has been.

■

Each step I took toward learning how to look at the homosexuality of my child left me stronger. I'm more certain of what I believe in, of what I consider important, and of what I need. I feel more independent because I'm taking responsibility for myself. When I first found out, I felt devastated. Now I feel tough.

SIX

TAKING A STAND AND TELLING OTHERS

*N*obody must know—it's nobody's business but ours. What if the neighbors find out?

It would kill the grandparents. They're so old they couldn't possibly understand.

We don't talk about the sex life of our nongay children, so why should we talk about the sex life of our gay child?

Such comments and thoughts during early grief sent parents into a self-imposed prison of silence. Somehow we perceived that we and our children had broken a societal law. We saw ourselves as guilty of creating and being part of an unacceptable portion of society. There was no trial. Our guilt was self-judged, and we found that the prison door slammed shut with surprising speed and force. Opening that door and coming out was a long arduous process. It involved taking yet another risk. We had to go beyond changing our own inner views. To gain a new order of personal freedom, we had to take a stand against the prevailing views of this society.

We could not really accept our children without taking such a stand inwardly and, later, outwardly. Parents who love their children and yet try to appease society through elaborate secrecy usually do not find this fence-straddling at all satisfactory. It leaves the gay children feeling not understood, accepted or loved for what they truly are.

Words are the connecting link between our inner feelings and society. They teach us and control us. They taught us the old ways about homosexuality. But the power goes both ways. If we are to break out of our fear and silence, we have to risk uttering our own new words. They are the key to personal freedom. Without the telling, we can't have the freedom.

So, for parents, coming out and taking a stand involves verbally supporting a gay or lesbian child either directly or indirectly to someone else in society. This covers a wide variety of supportive statements and activities from disagreeing with negative comments to making television appearances. There are no hard and fast rules for what a parent should do to come out. Some parents work publicly while many others work on the grassroots one-to-one level. The common denominator is that in one way or another, parents speak out.

Whenever a parent is able to say, "I have a gay or lesbian child" to anyone outside the immediate family, there is an underlying message: "As his or her parent, whatever befalls my child befalls me. I will fight with and for my child, for we are intertwined in our history and in our love for each other. My child is not alone. I stand with him or her."

In various ways, parents recognized and expressed the significance of taking a stand in the following quotes:

The more I come out and the more I face my own feelings, revealing them to people I trust, the less depressed I am. I would say that now I have no depression about my daughter's being gay. I don't think any more, "Isn't it too bad?"

■

There is a strain in any relationship if one person has to cover up something that's important. In fact, it's deadly.

■

When other people say, "Why tell anyone?" they just don't understand. There's something about the telling process that makes you feel whole.

■

When my son first told me, I said, "I hope you're not going to tell anyone else." Then I began to realize that I couldn't impose that rule on him. We've all taught our children not to lie, yet we're tempted to say to our gay children, "Don't lie exactly, but live a lie."

■

We parents are a kind of bridge. We're a bridge between the closeted community and the larger community. Even though we're "tainted" by being associated with a stigmatized group, we're still a respected part of the larger, heterosexual majority.

The fact that we're risking "being tainted" or risking being identified with a stigmatized group gives us a certain kind of force that a group of, say, clergy might not have.

■

I don't always trust statistics, but I do believe that one out of every ten people is gay. When I'm in a group and they start talking negatively about gays, I'll say, "One out of every ten people is homosexual. Who is it in this group?" That usually shuts them up. It makes them think that they could be hurting someone unknowingly. They realize I'm not kidding. I don't like to shoot people down, but I would like them to regroup their thinking.

■

I think that those of us who are openly talking about gayness can give others a little courage to do it. We have found that once you start speaking out, it isn't bad at all. I was scared at first. I didn't know how people were going to react, so I was very much on the defensive. I gave explanations on the latest research and so on. But now, if it comes up in conversation with somebody that I think really needs to know because I care about them or they care about me, I just tell them, period.

It is threatening to find ourselves, mild-mannered and law-abiding citizens, in a predicament involving conflicting values. Our dependency on society is usually subconscious until we have either broken or are unsure of the rules. We blame society, we submit to society, we love society, and we want to be an acceptable part of society. It is both "out there" and within us, contained in all our imprinted inner messages.

Taking a stand against society's injunctions is not to be taken lightly. In a sense, society understandably places pressure on us all to accept its rules of right and wrong. Through generations of experience, it has discovered many things that make human life good. Since we enjoy the benefits of society, it expects our allegiance. It offers painful penalties to nonconformers. But human life is not static. Change is necessary when new facts and situations call for a legitimate challenge to established ways.

Courage, self-awareness, and spirit are required of anyone who is challenging the status quo. When parents come out, we must first see society's disapproval as a condition somewhat of our own making. Only then can our inner belief system be questioned, clarified, and changed. Inner acceptance of gayness makes it easier to take a stand; and taking a stand causes us to feel acceptance at a gut level. We remain in self-imposed exile if we are so intimidated by fear of societal rejection that we stay ambivalent and silent.

The consequences of speaking up are usually less than we fear. When we come out of our suffocating cocoon of fear of "them" and what "they" think, we become our own persons. There is no greater prize we can win for ourselves.

Each time parents enter into a discussion with someone, somewhere, concerning homosexuality, we connect our inner feelings to someone else in the society. We in some way alter, both internally and externally, the prevailing prejudice. We often experience a sense of relief, and it whets our desire to speak out again. We have a sense of being in close touch with reality, and we are reinforced by the knowledge that each revelation brings us closer to our children.

The simplicity of this idea disguises the difficulty of the action. Parents move in and out of being able to talk. Whom to tell, when to tell, if to tell, why and what to tell become daily questions. Each of us develops an individual style of coping. Psychological comfort increases, and the telling is therapeutic whether or not those being told respond positively. The primary value of telling is in being real.

There are some wonderful parents who are totally out of the closet. I know one, and she says the first five years she didn't tell one soul. The last five years, she's been out everywhere. I think for most parents, it's been a step-by-step process.

■

I have found it such a good experience to tell people. Particularly for parents who are hurting, I want to say "Tell the people you trust! It's wonderful for your mental health." But there are some who cannot bring themselves to tell a single person. As a result, it seems to eat them up because they are going on the assumption that the other person is going to disapprove. It's like living with that person's severe disapproval when you haven't yet received it. You've got all the torments of disapproval and rejection without ever having put it to the test. You have nothing to lose by telling, because you're already in misery.

And the fact is that 95 times out of 100, if you tell the people that you care about and who care about you, and tell them in a positive way, they

*are going to be not only supportive, but closer to you because you shared
something important with them.*

■

*Fear can have tremendous power over us. We give that fear the power to
control us. When parents build this up into a dreadful secret, it becomes
something that has power over them. But once they confront it and talk
about it, even if they get a bad reaction, which is unlikely, at least they feel
they are being themselves.*

*It's such a good feeling to be yourself. Our children had the courage to
be themselves, when they came out to us. And we should have courage too.
It's a tremendous feeling. When you're being yourself, you don't have to
account to anybody anymore. You're free.*

Like children who test out their muscles and physical strength
as their maturation develops, parents will come out when their
emotional well-being is ready. We connect first with the people we
feel safest with, then with people we are not so sure of.

Parents who stand against the common view did not just wake
up one day and say, "I don't agree with these ideas. I will go out
and speak for my child." When we chose to leave the cell of silence,
we had to face that first "leap into decision," like the moment before deciding to make the first spring off the diving board. We recall the fear of the water, the urge to go to the edge, the retreat
down the ladder, and finally the moment of taking the plunge. Either we go or we don't.

For parents of gays, those feelings are the same, but the movement is usually more cautious. First we jump in from the side of
the pool, being careful to hold our nose. Only later do we jump
from the lowest and then, it is to be hoped, the highest of the
boards.

Standing against the prevailing view involves several stages of development:

■ Facing our inner fear of going against society's homophobia.

- Openly acknowledging to a few trusted others that we are parents of gay people. (Some parents never feel a need to come out beyond this point.)
- Beginning to speak out in the public arena, in protected and friendly places.
- Telling potentially critical others who need to become educated.
- Engaging with other parents in public forums and media events where some in the audience are known to be unsympathetic or uninformed.

Slowly we began to tell a few people. We had told a minister. I had told a therapist. We had both talked to several people at the Metropolitan Community Church, and they were very understanding. They did not seem to be put off by my fears of what people would think. Then I told my brothers and sisters, and they all responded without any great surprise or shock. They were all supportive. Then I began to tell a few close friends. In all these cases, there was no bad reaction. In fact, I would say there was an improved feeling between myself and whoever I told. It was as if a barrier had come down. In several cases, they told us that they had a gay child or relative.

In addition to the healthy need to be real, there are a variety of other motives for telling. We parents speak because we, too, feel the personal pain of being in a stigmatized minority, and we hate having to bear a penalty alone. We speak because we question the fairness of the stigma. We properly want justice for our children and ourselves. Finally we speak because we want to work to change the prejudice of society. We have learned that our negative inner messages are merely antiquated judgments based on a lack of truth. We have a deep desire to correct a misinformed society. This is how human society has been changed throughout history.

Dean, one of the men in my five-member carpool, is a good friend and has known about my son's gayness for several years. We were approaching my house on the Friday my wife and I were going to the second interna-

tional convention of Parents FLAG when Dean said, "Well, Rod, have a good time in the Big Apple."

Someone else asked, "You're going to New York this weekend? What for?"

After a couple of seconds' hesitation, I said, "Carolyn and I are going to a national convention of Parents, Families and Friends of Lesbians and Gays. My oldest son is gay." I got out of the car immediately after that and nothing else was said, but I went to New York feeling like a million dollars. Since then I have told several people at work—making sure they know it's no secret. It won't be a problem anymore for me to talk about it, and I want you to know it's liberating. The sky didn't fall in, no friends dropped me, and as far as I can tell, it hasn't changed a thing—except that now I don't have to keep quiet. I can make statements about the subject and give out information that people need to know. I recommend it highly. It only took me eight years.

■

I learned through my relationship with my daughter that when you share some tough things together, it brings you closer. You know, we all go around with our protection, with our "onionskin," so people can't get near the part of us that's vulnerable. We don't want people to know too much about us for fear we'll get hurt.

When I got into the parents' group, a big "onionskin" came off. I found I could be my real self and talk freely, and say the things I couldn't yet say in other places. That's a big relief and is probably the main reason for the group's success. It provides a nurturing setting, so the therapeutic effects of telling and sharing can take place.

When we see the healing effects of revealing our real selves in a protected situation, we can then risk being real in an unprotected setting. And we find that that, too, is healing and validating, no matter how it turns out.

■

We parents erroneously think, "If I don't tell anyone, then no one will know." In fact, parents may be literally the last to know, because of their need to screen out what they perceive to be dangerous information.

How much better it is when we finally can say, "Yes, my child is gay. He or she came into the world with that destiny. There is no fault. I will not accept the prejudice."

■

When we keep the gayness of our son or daughter a big secret, we assume our friends or relatives haven't already figured it out for themselves. In fact, they may know a lot and just aren't letting on.

■

I don't go around tapping people on the shoulder and saying, "I'm going to tell you something." Because it's nobody's business unless it is somebody who is important in our relationship, or unless I feel that telling will do some good. For example, I'm finding that I bring it up much more often if I feel that the conversation is moving to a point where negative comments are going to be made about minority groups, whether it be gays or women or different nationalities. This was a hard decision to make, but the more I talk about it, the easier it gets.

Frequently it will come up if someone asks me what I'm doing that evening. And I'll say, "I'm going to a support group that I belong to. It's Parents, Families and Friends of Lesbians and Gays. Gary is gay, you know." Then there may be a comment, like one of my friends who said, "Oh, I'm sorry." I said, "Well, what are you sorry about?" She replied, "Well, I just feel sorry for someone who will never have children, never have a happy life." Then I said, "Now you're doing what I did. You are projecting your idea of what happiness is onto somebody else. Gary is perfectly happy. So you don't have to feel sorry for him. I don't feel sorry for him. He's one of the happiest people I know." Her expression changed and she said, "I didn't know that."

I have many friends from church, and most of them are pretty naïve as to what gayness means. They desperately need to be educated, and I intend to do just that, but in a nonjudgmental way.

Most of the time, when parents reveal that their child is gay or lesbian, they are greeted with courtesy, warmth, and interest. Occasionally there is a sign of discomfort or the other person may change the subject.

Things are very similar when speaking before groups. We usually get great respect and courtesy from the audience. Occasionally there may be a person present whose religion or background

causes him or her to be hostile. When this happens, we listen carefully and then state that we do not pretend to have all the answers.
But we don't back down.

*There were a couple of people I told who didn't respond badly, but they
kind of changed the subject as soon as they could. They weren't comfortable.
I'm hoping they'll think about what I told them, but it's their problem. I intend to bring it up again because these people are relatives I see often.*

*Over the months I've told more and more people. Jack and I have talked
in front of many groups. The people seemed eager for information and tuned
in to us in a healthy way. I felt very authentic and close to those people. It
was almost a mystical experience for me. So I've gotten a lot out of speaking, and I want to do more.*

■

*I decided it was time to branch out and tell a few more people. My brother
is married to a woman who was rather forward-thinking and very broad-
minded, or so I thought. I told her about Don.*

*She said, "He isn't going to have surgery, is he?" This just threw me.
She's a social worker with a degree, and she should know something about
sexuality.*

*I said, "What do you mean?" Then she said, "Doesn't he want to be a
woman?" She's always thought that gay men wanted to be women, and
women wanted to be men. So I educated her. She really was totally ignorant.*

*Then I decided I'd tell my sister. Her remark was that it was all right
with her and that she still wanted to be friends with Don as long as he didn't
flaunt it. I asked her what she meant by that. And she said, "Well, act real
prissy and all."*

*I said, "Has he ever before?" She admitted that he hadn't. I said, "I don't
think he'll start doing it just because you know." Both these people have
since come around to an accepting point of view.*

There is an unspoken message conveyed when we speak for our
gay children. It is that homosexuality doesn't need to be hidden
or hushed up. Whether they know it or not, everyone has gay and

lesbian relatives or friends within their family, business or friend-ship circles. Each time parents speak out, they're helping all these people.

Telling others brings homosexuality home to people. When we as parents talk about our own children, it reminds others of the gay people they may know. It is hard to hate someone you know and care for. It is even harder to permit the denial of civil rights to a member of your own family or friendship circle.

I think of things I've done that scared me but that led to good feelings and growth. In the early years I was nervous about going places where I would see and speak before large groups of gay people such as the Metropolitan Community Church or Dignity, a Catholic support group. The culture says, "Don't get mixed up with gays." It implies, "You may be contaminated."

In actuality, I saw the people I met as being mirror images of my son and me. They showed appreciation, directly and indirectly, for our being there. We helped them with their parents, and they helped us understand our children. We came to admire them as human beings, and came to be outraged at the suffering they endured simply for being who they are: decent, responsible people who happened to belong to what society deemed an "out" group.

Parents can be held back by their own invisible nets of fear and oppression. Tuna fishermen report that dolphins are often accidentally trapped in the tuna nets. The dolphins could easily escape. The nets offer no real challenge to the dolphins' athletic abilities. But they become "frozen" and give up. These intelligent animals often die needlessly as they are pulled in with the tuna. I think parents kind of die inside when they can't get out of their own nets.

We long for society to change without our confrontation. But it doesn't work that way. The need for scapegoats and victims seems deep-rooted in those who have not faced their own sub-merged insecurities and resentments. We can have freedom for ourselves and our children only when we resolutely challenge oppressive bigotry. There is no substitute for courage and the will to act. Pastor Martin Niemöller reminds us of what can happen if we wait for others to do the work.

> In Germany the Nazis came for the Communists, and I didn't speak up because I wasn't a Communist. Then they came for the Jews, and I didn't speak up because I wasn't a Jew. Then they came for the trade unionists, and I didn't speak up because I wasn't a trade unionist. Then they came for the Catholics, and I didn't speak up because I was a Protestant. Then they came for me, and by that time no one was left to speak up.[1]

The decision to speak up is the measure of our commitment. Each time we tell another human being about having a gay or lesbian child, we take a step away from our own prejudice. A parent summarizes both the anxiety and satisfaction of learning to tell:

I started by telling people I felt sure of—people who would not reject me. These were people I trusted very much.

At first I told them only of my pain. I wanted to feel their sympathy. I didn't really care what they thought or believed. Gradually, as my outlook changed, I wanted to make sure they had their facts straight. I found many of them had incorrect information, as I once had, so then my goal became to educate them and change their view.

Each time I told someone, I felt queasy, unsure, and frightened beforehand because I didn't know what reaction I was going to get. Each time I felt much better afterward, whether the reaction was wholehearted support, which it often was, or an uncomfortable changing of the subject. I think every act of telling develops confidence even if it's at the elementary level of asking for sympathy.

In spite of considering myself out of the closet, and being proud of that fact, I still find myself in certain situations where I feel the desire to hide the fact that I have a gay child. This feeling always surprises me. The way I have handled this is to acknowledge that I still have some feelings I'm not proud of—feelings of homophobia. So the next time I'm in a similar situation, if I am able to speak up, to tell about my daughter in a positive way, in a way that is filled with pride in her, then I am really exhilarated.

I had been for so long controlled by what I thought other people's opinions were, that I found it incredibly freeing to act on what my opinion was. Actually, I never had a bad experience from the people I told, and now, if I did, it wouldn't bother me much.

Having felt, even a few times, the freedom of moving away from damaging conformity, I started taking some public actions. Today I am more and more openly political.

I now appear on television and radio. I make public speeches for gay rights and have my picture in the paper. I will not tolerate any negative comments against gay people in my presence. I feel anger and real disgust at homophobic statements and jokes, even though I myself sat in helpless silence only a few years ago.

Maybe it sounds saccharine, but I feel it's a real privilege to fight for something I believe in. I'm in it for myself too, you know, not just for others. All of us will have a better life when we don't have to put any group down in order to feel okay about ourselves. If parents don't speak out, then they're part of the problem. Maybe that's too judgmental. Let's say I want parents to progress to the point where they'll be able to speak openly about their own child and for the rights of all gay persons. It takes a long time to get to this point. It isn't easy to get there. Many parents don't get that far, but they continue to grow. Once you're in this thing, there's no end to your growing.

Some parents may not be political, but they are supportive and do a lot of good in a quiet way. If every gay person in our society felt accepted by his or her parents, there would be no "gay problem." Parents shouldn't feel bad if they go only as far as accepting their own child. They've had to change to get to that point. The door is open for movement that can come about later with changing circumstances.

NOTE FOR CHAPTER SIX

1. John Bartlett, *Familiar Quotations* (Boston: Little, Brown and Co., 1980), p. 824.

I have no qualms about accepting my son. I love him as much as ever. But now my husband and I are in the closet. We cannot share this with our families. If we were invited to my only brother's house, and my son wanted to bring his friend, whatever would I say?

■

S E V E N

■

THE REST OF THE FAMILY

Whether they are explicitly told about it or not, the grandparents, siblings, aunts and uncles, in-laws and cousins, will all be affected directly or indirectly by the gayness of a family member. Those who know will have to explore their values, their fears, their commitment. Those who don't know are apt to sense a barrier, an unhappy change in family dynamics; this will undoubtedly be disturbing to them.

The choice whether to tell the rest of the family is usually placed on the shoulders of the parents. No matter which choice they make there will be pain. They can withdraw from their extended families into pain and isolation. They may say nothing and limit conversation to the familiar banalities as if no important change had happened, and expect their gay child to do likewise. Or they can open up their pain and consider new possibilities. In our contact with parents, and in our interviews, we have seen these three basic reactions, even though they come disguised in fifty-seven varieties.

Parents gave a great deal of energy and thought to other family members. Over and over, parents wrestled with questions about their families. They were concerned about how everyone would view them as parents. And they were concerned about any adverse effect the news would have on individual members.

The wide range of responses that came out in our interviews touched a variety of personal and family situations. These taught us that no parent is alone in his or her reaction. Also, by getting in touch with a range of reactions, we can see the struggles within the family with more compassion.

Some of our married respondents shared information about how their marriage itself was affected. There were also discussions about the pros and cons of telling grandparents, siblings, aunts, and uncles. Parents shared how they handled the incorporation of the gay child's lover into the family. A gay man talked about some basic assumptions that have to be examined before families can come to terms with their homophobic feelings. And fortunately, we were able to interview several siblings of the gay children. These siblings gave us a good picture of the seesaw effect, the early pulling apart and then drawing together, that was typical of so many accepting families.

EFFECT ON THE MARRIAGE

In the case of married parents, our interviews showed that the marriage itself was affected when the couple faced the fact of having a gay child. As each person felt his or her grief, change and tension occurred within the relationship. Some couples reported feeling more united as they joined together in shaking old beliefs.

But the more prevalent reaction was a kind of separateness during the initial mourning period. Each person felt alone as old frictions were aggravated and new ones added.

With time, however, the couple settled into a day-by-day adjustment to their grief. Their pain lost some of its intensity, and they began to turn again toward each other. When one spouse made a move toward acceptance, he or she was often able to help the other make the same move.

Ruth and I have had some uncomfortable discussions about Debby's gayness. Ruth needs to talk about things that are bothering her. I tend to "clam up" and try to reason things out within myself rather than discuss them openly. This has created problems. And because we first thought parents were the cause, we spent a lot of time blaming ourselves and each other. We hurt one another over this.

■

Sometimes I feel bad about my relationship with my husband. I'm not comfortable talking to him about Mary, so we don't talk about it much. He thinks there's nothing to talk about. She's gay. That's it. There's nothing he can do. He'll continue loving her and seeing her during holidays and whenever. But he'll never mention it to her. Those are his wishes. I know it's painful for him, so his way of handling it is to ignore it. I think he'd probably burst into tears if we ever got into a deep discussion about Mary's being gay. But I don't want to handle it the way he does. Sometimes I feel pulled apart by this.

■

I realize we used the fact that Carrie is a homosexual as an excuse for not dealing with some of our other problems. Outwardly we seemed to be fighting over how to handle Carrie's gayness; but in truth we were having fights over things that didn't have anything to do with Carrie. For instance, the problems married people have when children leave home, the so-called empty-nest syndrome. We were going through that when Carrie told us she was gay. We let Carrie's situation keep us from dealing with the sadness and grief that we were feeling about the loss of our parent role, the mom-

and-dad role. I think it took us longer to be able to understand that loss, because we thought this gayness was the source of all our difficulties.

■

It's interesting that finding out Hal was gay didn't cause marital troubles for us. I think for most parents it does. It's a problem they don't need. We weren't getting along all that well, and we didn't need it either. We were both reared in troubled times and in troubled families. We both had the trappings of being well-adjusted, but when it came to living with someone else and nurturing that other spouse, we didn't have it.

So it was strange that learning about Hal's being gay didn't create a lot of problems with our relationship. Considering our lack of information and our need to present a good front, it should have. Somehow it seemed clear what we should do. Whereas we didn't always understand our own relationship, with this issue we understood each other. We knew we had to work on supporting each other and supporting Hal. We went in that direction. As each month passed, we handled it better and better.

I don't think we ever had quarrels over it. Oh, maybe some competition. Bob or I might say, "Well, I'm moving along with it a little faster than you." By and large we held together very well.

OTHER CHILDREN IN THE FAMILY

The people we interviewed had strong nuclear family relationships, whether they were married or not. They often spoke of the other members of the immediate family and how they were affected. We were impressed by certain elements of the interactions within the families. There were family rules, but the rules were flexible. Anger and disappointment were freely expressed, and individuality was accepted as the norm. Family pride, respect, and closeness were typical. In our talks with other gays and lesbians, many were not as fortunate as the gay children in these accepting families.

Most of our parents told their other children as soon as possible, since they knew that secrets were barriers to familial support and understanding. They felt their gay child deserved and needed the support of the family circle, and their other children needed to know what was going on. Very young children were not told until it was felt they could understand.

The children were torn by a mixture of feelings. Some teenage siblings were exposed to fierce inner pressures—"Will my brother's being gay somehow rub off on me? Will they think I'm a lesbian?" Caught in their own personal crises, they were unable to offer much support.

On the other hand, many older siblings tended to play a helpful role. Often these older siblings were the first to know and acted as understanding intermediaries between the parents and the gay member. A good rule of thumb seems to be: If the gay child's siblings got along well with him or her before the coming out, they will usually continue to do so afterward. If the relationships were never close, or were strained, coming out can become another bone of contention. In other words, the initial reactions will be affected by factors such as the age of the children, family traditions, and the nature of the relationships in each family.

Parents recalled how their other children reacted:

My gay son, Gary, is very close to his older brother Pete, who is twenty months older. Pete has always taken care of Gary. They were together constantly. I didn't know how Pete would react. He's not macho, but he's associated with a lot of fellows who are. While he's very loving, sweet and compassionate, I'd say Pete was always much more into sports and athletics and all the stereotypical things that males do.

After things settled down a bit, I got a chance to talk to Pete about his reaction. He said, "I have no problem with that at all. I love Gary more than any person in the world. He's still Gary—he's still my brother."

Then he said something that showed me I had an irritated older son who was really hurt that we would even for a moment question how he would react. He said, "I do get tired of people always wanting to know how I'm going to handle Gary's gayness. Dad, how did you think I was going to react? What do you think of me? How could you think I would hurt my own brother!"

■

Our other children had no problem accepting the fact that Rich is gay. The news was no "big deal," and they are all comfortable with it now. One of our sons was a worry for us. Eric is the macho type and had made some derogatory remarks at times about gays. When Rich told him, Eric was very accepting. It didn't bother him at all, and he's been great about it ever since. So our worries were pointless. I think it speaks for the maturity and the close family feeling that the children have for each other. Nothing is going to break that up!

■

Andy came out to his married sister before he told me. Even though she was very accepting and her attitude was good, my daughter was under a strain until I found out too. But she was very helpful in her responses to him. Once when he was upset because he hadn't found a special person, she said, "Andy, you can't look for a person so intensely. It's like trying to catch a butterfly. If you're watching, it'll never happen. But if you're not, the butterfly might sit on your shoulder." After that, he didn't seem to have that feeling of urgency and was more satisfied.

THE SIBLINGS SPEAK

The observations just presented were accounts by parents as to how they saw their other children responding. Now we want to present some accounts, at greater length, by the sisters and brothers themselves. All of the incidents, except the first one, involve siblings who were in their early teen years when they found out.

As we listened to these and other children in our families, we noticed some common initial reactions:

- Older siblings (past their teen years) who were secure in their sexual identity had fewer problems with the news. Those who had the experience of having gay and lesbian friends were able to see the situation in terms of the larger social issues.

- Some siblings who found out during their stressful teen years expressed a feeling that the gay child was responsible for shattering the image of a "perfect" family.
- Teenagers may also have felt a loss of parental support when their parents were in the early stages of their own grief.
- Some youngsters feared being verbally (or even physically) attacked by their peers.
- For many teenagers, learning of the sibling's gayness triggered questions about their own sexuality. Fearing and questioning their own sexuality is a very common occurrence for young people as well as for their parents. It is a threat because in the early stages they see gayness as a handicap at best and as an affliction at worst.

All of these reactions and feelings were worked through as the teens underwent a learning process remarkably similar to their parents.

Valerie

Valerie was in her middle twenties when her younger brother came out to her. Her age and wide range of experiences were major factors in her early and total acceptance of her brother's gayness. She is a person who sees the political aspects of our society's antigay attitudes.

For me it wasn't hard when Chris came out, because a lot of my friends have been lesbians and gay men. I feel really positive about people who are gay or lesbian. The sickness or health of a relationship has to be judged by what is going on between the two people. I judge a couple by whether there is mutual respect and whether the people are growing in the same direction. It's also important whether a relationship helps people take responsibility for what's going on in society or whether it's just a nice comfy place that helps people not deal with society's problems.

For many of the women I know, coming out was a positive thing. These couples seemed to care more about each other and were more open with each other than most heterosexual couples. They weren't worried about looks or power or whatever. That made a lot of sense to me. My experiences with the gay men and lesbians I know have made me question society's antigayness and the thinking that there's something wrong or sick about loving someone of the same sex.

Valerie then talked about what she saw as the source of much parental misinformation and guilt. Her awareness showed an ability to empathize with the feelings and needs of others.

One day I was in a grocery store line and picked up a woman's magazine that offered advice to parents of gays. It criticized parents by repeating the classic stereotyped thinking that distant fathers and domineering mothers produce sick children. People who get their information from articles like that would, of course, be very upset by their child's gayness. Reading such articles, it's no wonder that parents feel something is dreadfully wrong and that it's all their fault.

For many gay people and their parents it's a process of groping past all the antigayness that's around. Gay men and lesbian women have to affirm what they naturally want to do, or what they've decided to do, depending on the person.

She discussed ideas that might help parents come to terms with their grief and closed her interview with a hope for the future.

I've seen my mom and dad struggle with letting all of us live our own lives. They know their children aren't six years old anymore and are going to follow their own paths. I believe it would help all parents to keep this idea as their bottom line and to remind themselves of that often. No amount of fretting will change it.

I think it's important for parents to understand how much of their disappointment about their child's coming out is due to the antigay propaganda that we're flooded with, and how much of their disappointment might also come from wanting to relive their own lives through their child. It seems to me that a lot of parents want their child to have a wedding just so they can share that experience with their friends. For a while my parents wanted that too. But they reconsidered and decided they wanted a more real and honest relationship with their friends. I remember their saying, "Well, those friends who are truly close will know and understand. Those who are judgmental and antigay don't matter to us anyway. So, too bad for them." This sort of thinking would help all parents.

You know, everybody concerned would be helped if society could begin to understand why it is so antigay. If everyone could view homosexual relationships with a more open mind, the stigma attached to being gay would be reduced. The gay movement has begun to spread this idea among people. It's a little like the way the women's movement spread the idea among millions of people that women should be respected and shouldn't have to accept a secondary position. The whole society will be better as women are appreciated and as gay people are appreciated.

Susan

Susan was a junior in high school when her brother, six years her senior, told her he was gay. She felt torn to some extent by the news. But by examining her innermost perceptions, she was able to resolve her conflict. As she became more independent, she became a quiet champion of her family's effort to improve society's image about gayness.

After my brother told me he was gay, I had feelings of disappointment that he wasn't an "ideal" brother. I think that was caused partly by my own desire to be "ideal," sort of perfect. If he wasn't perfect, it really affected my feelings about whether I was okay or not. I asked myself, "Could I be gay too?"

Knowing about Chris made me in some ways more willing to deal with people who I knew were gay. Before, I probably would have just shut them out. Beyond that, I don't really think the fact that he was gay affected me. It didn't make me feel that the family was weird. In fact, I felt good about the way we handled it, when we finally got around to talking about it. I think I was probably too caught up in my own life, trying to be more independent and that kind of thing, to focus on my brother's gayness. It wasn't as much of an upheaval for me as it was for my parents. In some ways I think it was good because it made us talk about things that we really hadn't talked about before.

Susan was candid in discussing her occasional wish for the problem not to "be." We were glad that she brought it up. It is a wish that is almost universal in families when the members are faced with tough problems.

There have been times when I have wished Chris weren't gay. Sometimes I have feelings of wanting the family to be more average. Like when we get together with the cousins, and they talk about their engagements and having children, and so forth. There's a part of that that is really appealing. So sometimes I do want that. I want something that's a little bit closer to average.

But I don't think it's his being gay that bothers me as much as some elements of his personality. In other words, I have issues with him that are not centered around gayness.

She showed concern about taking or not taking a stand for gays and lesbians.

I don't feel free to talk about my brother. Partly it's because I was never quite sure how Chris felt about my just coming right out and saying, "Yes, my brother's gay." Especially when I am with people who might know him. Several years ago I mentioned it to some people who knew him, and he told me, "I prefer that you not say that." So I stopped telling anyone except close friends about it. But now it seems like I am basically open with people who will be respectful of the information. I might mention it to them, if it comes up.

There have been times when I've said, "I don't like gay jokes," or "I don't like your saying that." I'm more willing to stand up for gay people, and I think that's good. Every once in a while if someone jokes about gays, and I think that person is receptive, I'll say, "Well, my brother is gay and I love him, so if you make fun of gay people, you're making fun of somebody I care about. I don't like that and I don't think you would either if you were in my place." Then sometimes I'll tell them all about it. But I don't really make a big cause out of it.

Denny

Denny was fifteen years old when he found out for sure that his brother, Craig, was gay. He was struggling with all the usual developmental problems of a boy his age and then had to suffer through what most people in the immediate families of gays and lesbians fear will happen but usually doesn't. He endured open and hard ridicule from his peers and suffered a loss of status. Even so, he made significant changes in his attitude toward gay people and continues to do so. The brothers are now close friends, and Craig was best man at Denny's wedding. At the time of our interview, Denny was twenty-two.

I had heard some kidding about Craig's being gay from a guy in the band, but I was still pretty shocked and surprised when Craig told us. I was upset, you know, sort of grieving. It seemed like there was an end to my idea of what "normal" is. I had thought that our whole family was perfectly normal, but Craig's being gay was abnormal. To me the norm is straight.

At school I was treated like I was gay too. The kids would holler that Craig and I were both fags. They would do that on the bus or at band practice—any public place where they thought they could ridicule me. One day I just got fed up with it and hit one of them. That stopped him and the other nasty kids as well.

There was another reason why they shut up too. I was going wild with women then. It was a good move for me to show how heterosexual I was for a while. It was the logical thing to do. The next year, after Craig graduated, the whole thing died down.

In the next section, there is searching for the reason for the homophobia that hurt him.

People act terrible when they're stupid and ignorant and afraid. And the kids in my class were stupid and ignorant and afraid about homosexuality. It's the guys that will give you trouble. They all called each other queer. The guys were very afraid they could turn into homosexuals. Except me. I really don't have any homosexual tendencies. I've always been fascinated by females. I've never had the problem of being worried about being gay.

The problems that Denny had at school were not his only concerns about his brother's gayness.

You have a crisis when your idea of what the world is doesn't fit what it actually is. The closer you are to the part that doesn't fit, the more of a shock it will be. You have a family crisis when someone is not what you thought they were.

Craig's a smart guy, and he's strong. He's my older brother, and everything he does has meaning to me. His being gay just wasn't in my picture of him. You know, it threatens your entire system when something like this happens. It threatens your whole belief in the world. You're not sure of anything. When things aren't what they seem, it's a big shock.

I had to deal with my feelings about my brother. He does not look at girls in the same way that I look at girls. I would rather that he had been more like me—that we could have done some stuff together. I lost any chance of searching for girls with my brother, which would have been fun. Since we weren't the same, that was something I missed out on.

Denny talked about the rest of his family members. Even with the pain he was subjected to by insensitive peers, he made a significant adjustment.

Mom and Dad cried a lot, yelled a lot, and went to group meetings. Dad moped around. Both of them spent a lot of time blaming themselves. They didn't pay much attention to me. For a while there it seemed like I lost them.

Still, we all accepted Craig's being gay instead of hoping he would change. We didn't hide anything about it from ourselves. Mom and Dad had made sure that we all knew, and I think that was a good idea.

I didn't help Craig much at first. I was too busy coping with it myself. I wasn't ready to help him. I was only fifteen. It's not realistic to expect someone of that age to do much. Craig talked to me some and asked me how I was doing. When he did that, I did try to reassure him. As time went on, I felt better and wanted to understand him. He was different even when he and I were growing up. He didn't like to play sports, and he didn't go outside for recess. And he never said he didn't like girls. I think that was because girls just never were that important to him.

I would change Craig if I could, as I believe he would change himself. I don't want either of us to hurt anymore. But I certainly wouldn't want to change all gays. In reality, being gay is not a problem except for how we cope with it. Gays are just another group of interesting people. They have a different perspective on life. Gays don't make me nervous the slightest bit.

Jane

Jane, Denny and Craig's sister, was thirteen when she received the news that her oldest brother was gay. She is the youngest and the only daughter in her family. Her early experience after Craig came out was different from Denny's, but nevertheless there was a period of adjustment for her. Jane, who was nineteen when we interviewed her, began her discussion of how the news affected her with the usual "finding out."

Craig called a family conference to tell us about his being gay. But I didn't realize what it meant. I had no idea how bad it was on Craig or Mom and Dad. The only bad effect it had on me directly was that it made me scared that I might be gay also. I worried about that off and on for months—really until I had sex with a boy and found out how much I liked it. (She laughs.) *I don't want my dad to hear this.*

Jane's school experience was less dramatic than her brother's. However it was not without problems.

I didn't have trouble at school the way Denny did. In fact, for a long time I didn't even know how badly Denny was being hassled. The kids who were bothering Denny were being nice to me. I never have figured out why they were nice to me, but mean to him. It was kind of odd. But after I found out, I went to war with them. Nobody is going to say anything about my brothers and get by with it.

I had a chemistry teacher who was always making comments in class about "fags and queers." That was hard to take. But I tried to consider the source. She was also very seductive with the fourteen-year-old boys in the class. If she had been more intelligent and nicer it would have been harder to deal with her stupidity, but she wasn't a wonderful person. So it was easy for me to just hate her.

I was pretty emotional about the school thing for a while, and I turned into a self-righteous liberal. For a long time I was furious about the way people feel about homosexuality. Then I realized that they are ignorant about it, the way I used to be—just totally ignorant.

The effects on the family life are sometimes dramatic. Jane found a near reversal of roles as she comforted the other family members.

I didn't go around thinking everything was hunky-dory about my family like I had before. Everyone was unhappy, and that made it hard to deal with. We were still close. We still cared. But people weren't as much fun. More than one of us was unhappy at any given time. There were outbursts, and I would try to get people to feel better.

I was sometimes impatient about my parents' blaming themselves. I wished they would just accept it and go on with their lives. It was hard for me to know what to say or to understand everything they were feeling. But everyone was hurting, and I tried to help by listening and reassuring.

I never wished that Craig weren't gay. I think he's just fine like he is— except that he does overspend. He'll do well at a job with no problems at all. I sometimes worry about his having sex with too many people. I'm afraid he could get venereal disease or worse.

For a while he had a lover, a partner. I spent time with them. It was just a relationship to me. At first, seeing them hug was kind of hard. But not for long. You can't hate love between two people. His love affair made me feel good. He was happy. I guess if you're worried about your own sexuality, you might hate to see two males or two females touching in a sexual way. If you're sure of your own sexuality and you see it over a period of time, it becomes a normal thing.

Craig and his lover were a part of our family. When they broke up, I felt like I would if anyone I cared about got a divorce. I hurt for Craig, because I knew he was going through a hard time. I felt sad for him. I didn't think they'd ever break up. I felt we'd lost a family member, and I still really and truly like his ex-lover—a lot.

For Craig, being gay is a very deep thing. I know that to come out and say he was homosexual was the single hardest thing he's ever done. He told me about it. But homosexuality is right for him. He had to be who he is. I'm glad he told all of us.

I've learned a lot from all of this. Having a gay brother opened my mind to other people. I even understand conservatives better. I'm more tolerant.

As a family we hung in there. We didn't deny any part of our feelings. We didn't pretend we weren't hurting when we were. I believe you'll hurt the gay person a lot more if you don't face up to how you really feel. It may take years to learn and accept and to understand, but once you get there, it's worth it.

TELLING THE GRANDPARENTS

Bringing their own parents the news was one of the hardest tasks for parents. Parents viewed the grandparents as being vulnerable: "With their health problems, I just wouldn't want them to hear about this on top of everything else." Or as uninformed: "They are of a different generation, and they just couldn't understand or handle it." Or as possibly rejecting: "I wouldn't want my gay son or lesbian daughter to be looked on as an unacceptable person by his or her own grandparents."

As parents began to understand their own homophobia and worked at getting rid of it, the power of their reasons for not sharing with their parents dimmed. Many chose to include the grandparents in their family situation. A few parents let their parents know early in their grieving time, but on the whole this was not the case.

The grandparents who were told handled the information well. Though their knowledge about gayness was limited, they certainly knew what it was. The relationship between the grandparents and their children and grandchildren took on a renewed sense of togetherness. Their biological bond was fortified as they worked to understand what was happening.

Telling a Grandfather

My father was eighty-one years old when I told him about Bill. It had been worrying me for several years, and I finally told him. I guess I never would have if it had been easy not to. What I mean by that is that given the choice, I don't stick my neck out. I take the easy route. I avoid any controversy. But I have trouble telling lies. I have always prided myself on being honest, even if it made me look bad. Sometimes I think I go overboard. Anyway, it seems that when I can't be honest with people who mean something to me, a barrier goes up between them and me. I was beginning to dread seeing him because I couldn't be myself with him.

So I told him. And he said, "I'm glad you didn't tell your mother" (who had died several years earlier). I told him that I was sorry I hadn't because it had affected our relationship. I wasn't being honest with her about something that was extremely important to me. At least if I had told her, we would have understood each other better.

After he had some time to digest it, my dad began to talk more reasonably about it. I gave him some of the literature from our parents' group, and he read it.

Overall I think he took it pretty well. He still asks about Bill, and when he talked to him on the phone, he invited Bill to come and live with him if he got a job in his town. And whether he takes it well or not, I have it off my chest. It's my son and he's my father. We all need to be honest with each other. I felt closer to my dad after our talk, and he seemed to feel closer to me.

Telling a Grandmother

My seventy-four-year-old mother was planning to visit for three weeks last month. She didn't know about her grandson's homosexuality or about our involvement in Parents FLAG. My wife and I decided to avoid raising the possibility that this visit would be the time of her enlightenment. That meant writing to a few people to remove "Parents of Gays" from their mailing envelopes to our home (since we are both employed outside the home), not being able to answer the hot line, and telling a few folks that when they called we might not be able to talk freely. It also meant boxing up all the materials, books, pamphlets, and newsletters that cluttered my study.

We went to this extent—not because we are ashamed of our son or unwilling to discuss the matter with my mother—but because we had promised Michael that this topic was to be raised with family members at his initiative and on his terms. In fact, during the past four and one half years there *have been many times when I've wanted to be more open and honest with my mother. On the one hand, I had the feeling that she would understand, that her love for her grandson and our family could sustain her through any family crisis. But—to be perfectly honest—there was that nagging doubt: What if she finds out and rejects our wonderful son? Over the years, then, our visits with her have always created this mental game of ping-pong for me.*

Before Mother's arrival I said to my wife, "There's one letter addressed to 'Parents of Gays' that comes into the house two or three times a year that I can't change. The Internal Revenue Service will not send their tax exemption correspondence to a post office box; they send it only to a person's home. We'll just have to take that chance. If it comes in, and she asks about it, we'll tell the truth and take it from there."

Things went well for two weeks. My anxiety level lessened with each passing day. One day I came home from work to find the mail stacked on the kitchen counter—and the IRS letter was on top. My heart raced. From the living room I heard, "Tom, there's a letter that came in today that raises questions. Will you tell me about it and tell me the truth?" Her tone was soft, yet firm; one that I have known for almost fifty years. "Well, Mother," I said, "Sue and I are members of a wonderful group of parents who love and support their homosexual children. You have a gay grandson."

I sat down, and we talked for about two hours. It was evident that she was willing to try to understand. She asked many questions. I had so much to tell her that at times it just poured out. We agreed that in the remaining week of her visit she'd do some reading and we'd do more talking together. All this was so new to her.

As we talked, I began to realize that she hadn't said she still loved her grandson. I've always expected too much too soon from my parents. I needed to hear those words now. When they didn't come fast enough, I began to choke up. With tears in my eyes I blurted out, "Mother, it will be like putting a knife in my heart if you reject Michael. We love him so much." She reached over to hold my hand and assured me that she would never turn her back on him.

A little later we went to pick up Sue from work. When she got into the car, I told her that the IRS letter had arrived that afternoon. There was silence. "It's all right," Mother said. "There's no tragedy where there's love."

Aunts and Uncles

Where the immediate family is concerned, it is just about inevitable that some facing up to the issue will have to take place. But where other relatives are concerned, a different decision must be made. The generations that some of these relatives came from were exposed to much homophobia, so it is natural to have some reservations about telling them.

As parents and individuals we have ties and ego involvement with them. We were expected to accomplish in ways that would shed credit on the larger family. We have old rivalries with our brothers, sisters, and cousins. Will they consider us failures if we tell them about our gay child? Did we disgrace them? Will it cause serious upset, or worse? Will we be distanced? How will our gay child and his or her lover be received? What about the holidays?

At first glance, one might assume that our close relatives—our own parents, sisters, brothers, and cousins—would be a source of nurture. The blunt truth is, we can't count on it. Once again we confront the old questions. Should we stay in the closet? At what price—to ourselves, our child, and our immediate family?

Our general experience is that there is health and healing in telling the truth. But there can be exceptions. There is no substitute for trusting one's intuitions.

One parent told his sister, and six months later found out his sister also had a lesbian daughter:

After we found out, I told my sister within a few months. I told her we were struggling with it, but that we were making progress. She was completely supportive. A few months later, one of her own daughters told her that she was lesbian. The fact that I had talked to her about Anne had been a big help to her. When she got the news, she knew she wasn't alone.

■

At some point, I decided to write my sister and her husband that Jeannie was lesbian. I received a nice letter back saying they understood and that they had some gay acquaintances they liked. Later we went up to visit them for a weekend. In talking about our families, we mentioned Jeannie, and my sister said, "Why do you need to tell anyone?" Not the most awful remark, but somehow I felt from this and her other comments that she was disapproving. I know she is conservative on a lot of things, and I read into her remark that gayness would be better off not mentioned.

In letters I have written them since, I mention Jeannie and gay matters, but they don't respond to these topics. The truth is, our relationship was distant before Jeannie's lesbianism came up. It still is. Yet, I don't think telling hurt the relationship. It may even have helped it a little in other ways.

Sometimes a relative just "clams up," but later moves to a more open position. It may take them time to adjust just as it does parents.

Fairly soon after Sam told us, I decided to tell my brother. He is a warm, caring person and was close to Sam all the while he was growing up. He accepted the news easily. He sensed my pain and felt sympathy for the adjustment we had to make.

My wife and I would occasionally talk about Sam and his lover or mention gay issues or events. I noticed my sister-in-law never said anything in response. She is from a conservative religious tradition that might make homosexuality a forbidden subject, so I assumed she was uncomfortable with it and disapproving.

We decided to continue to mention the topic anyway. We did so casually but repeatedly over a period of years with the pattern remaining about the same. One of the nicest surprises I have had grew out of this situation. We had a special guest speaker at one of our parents' meetings. I invited my brother, and when he arrived for the meeting, his wife was with him. She took part in the rap groups and took an active, friendly role in interacting with both the parents and gay people there. She talked about how proud she was of her gay nephew. I was really grateful for the caring she showed and respected her making the decision to come.

A moral I drew from this: "Be careful about giving up on anyone's capacity to change." I know one result—it opened positive new feelings toward her for me and strengthened good feelings about the family.

Another parent described why she has chosen not to tell her own siblings.

I have not told members of my family such as my brothers and sisters. I've thought about it, and I'm still not telling them. I don't see them as being very open. I think I could tell at least one brother. I probably could tell all of them if I wanted to, but I still don't want to.

I think the people in our generation, people who are now in their fifties, sixties, and seventies, have a harder time than people in their thirties or forties. Many in our generation were taught that homosexuality, even divorce, and a lot of other customs were sinful and immoral. They have a very hard time changing their outlook. Come to think of it I don't remember homosexuality being talked about in my background. I never heard my mother or father ever mention it. They had other things to worry about during the depression. As far as homosexuality was concerned I was just totally unaware, and so were my brothers and sisters. I wasn't even very familiar with the word. I think I was well along in years before I knew there was such a thing.

Some of our parents found an enormous amount of help when they told their own sisters and brothers. The next quote is a good example of this.

The smartest thing I ever did was to tell my sister right away. Martha was there for all of us in every way. She knew about homosexuality, and she knew about feelings. She helped us sort through whatever was bothering us. When the children were confused and acting up, she was able to explain how they were feeling. There was a time when everyone in the family went off into separate corners. But she kind of grabbed hold of each of us and brought us back together. I don't think we'd have done nearly as well without her.

THE LOVERS

On the obstacle course toward acceptance, one of the hurdles is what to do about the lovers. Even though gay people may often use the word *partner*, the parents' ears hear *lover*. To parents, the word *lover* is prickly in itself. Its connotations are associated with the ideal of youthful, heterosexual romance. *Lover* goes with moon, spoon, June, bridal gown, and babies. *Lover* may also suggest illicit love. Long after parents have made peace with the reality of gayness, and even with the partner of the gay child, many still have trouble saying the word *lover*.

The truth is that we are dealing here with deep areas of parental resistance and residual homophobia. While we are undergoing all kinds of changes about our child's being gay, there rides along in some inner place a hope—a hope that maybe some miracle will happen and somehow our child will cease being gay. Acknowledging the sexual aspect of our child's life, and knowing his or her lover, causes that old unrealistic hope to fade rapidly.

Those of us who are fortunate enough to meet and get to know our child's lover generally report this as being a very positive experience. When we meet the lesbian or gay lover, and see how satisfying and happy is their relationship, we realize our child is not alone. We realize our child is not the only fine gay person in the world.

The first time John brought his lover home, there was an uneasiness for me, because I was worried that I might make him feel uncomfortable. It wasn't that I didn't want him to visit, or that I couldn't accept him. That didn't enter into it. I was fearful that I might make some statement very unintentionally that would make him feel unwelcome. But after the first time, there's been no problem at all.

Shortly after Amy told us, she invited her lesbian lover, Peggy, to come over. Even though she had been in our house many times before and knew we liked her, Peggy was obviously uneasy now that we knew she was a lesbian and our daughter's lover. We could see she was nervous. So when she came in, we hugged her and said, "Don't you worry for a moment over how we feel about you—we love you just like we did before." Peggy said she felt better and that she had been afraid we would hold her somehow responsible for Amy's being a lesbian. I don't know all that much about Amy's relationships, but as far as I know, this was Amy's first love affair with a girl. This friend had recognized her homosexuality several years before Amy had recognized her own, so she was afraid Amy's parents might say, "Well, you caused it." We assured her, "No, neither of us thinks that at all. Amy is still an individual and could have said no if she didn't feel that way toward you."

■

On the question of "Where will they sleep?" we personally lean toward the position that our children at some point in their maturity become guests in our house. We have the right to state the ground rules of our piece of turf—for the nongay children or the gay children. And we have the right to let the rules bend and evolve as the relationships evolve.

I know people differ on this matter because of religious traditions, or the way they were brought up. For ourselves, we give priority to fairness. We had to adjust to our heterosexual kids having "live-in" arrangements. We finally came around to letting them share a bedroom in our house. Fairness says the same principle should apply to our gay child and her lover.

■

I'm at the point in my acceptance where homosexuality has very little, if any, negative connotation to me. The sex idea has ceased to bother me. Somewhere along the line, I lost that. Pretty soon after our son formed that relationship with Marty, my uneasiness left. That relationship plus more knowledge helped. The more knowledge I gained, the easier I felt.

What did hurt us was when George and Marty broke up. Marty had become a familiar figure in our home. I had genuine, deep affection for him. When they decided to part, I had the feelings parents must have when one of their married children decides to divorce. I'm not absolutely certain what caused it to break up. The other man grew into a different person. That may be the reason. George said he wants a long-term relationship. I hope he'll find someone who complements him. I don't know what type of person that would be. I think one day he'll find someone.

We spoke with one gay man, Jonathan, who had given considerable thought to the problems faced by parents in extending total acceptance to their gay and lesbian children. He brought up some concerns that are rarely talked about but are often thought about.

After getting over their hope that we can change, most parents worry that we'll lead lonely, unhappy lives. So they hope we'll find a nurturing partner. One of the most oppressive things, for a gay man at least, is the pressure from parents to adopt a full-formed, marriage-type relationship. The pressure is for a discreet, lifelong relationship—if possible, with some very "successful" partner.

Parents seem to resist any idea of a couple relationship that is not modeled after the ideal of heterosexual marriage. The fact is that gay male couples may be devoted and loving, but they are sometimes, often with permission from one another, non-monogamous. Some devoted gay male couples are able to do this without damaging their primary relationship, but this is upsetting to most parents. Whether we like it or not, heterosexual couples are sometimes non-monogamous too, but they are more secretive about it.

There are so many double standards. The widespread deviation from "the ideal" by heterosexuals is taken in stride, but very similar actions by gays are viewed as shameful. In California, where I live now, marriages last on the average something like five to seven years. So the real world of heterosexuals is more like a string of serial relationships—with or without marriage. I even heard a woman at a Santa Monica cocktail party say, "Oh, she'll make a lovely first wife for him."

If gays change partners at some similar rate, parents view it with special sorrow and dismay. The implication is that gays are "just promiscuous," and can't have serious, prolonged relationships. The fact is that many of them do, and they are highly caring and loving. Though again, if it is not 100 percent monogamous, it is considered peculiar or destructive. Parents need to remember that gays are denied any legal or spiritual equivalent of marriage. Imagine the straight world under those circumstances.

When families get together at Christmas or other holidays, talk goes on about a breakup or divorce of this couple or that. But the breakup of a gay couple is viewed as unseemly and is given the old hush-hush treatment. So, as I say, if parents lay on us some unrealistic ideals which aren't lived up to even in the straight world—then to me it is oppression.

For example, a lot of gays are finding non-monogamous sex unsatisfy-ing. If they felt they would not be met with hurt or lectures, they would wel-come the chance to rethink freely this important part of their lives. They respect the life experiences of their parents, and they know their parents aren't saints. Maybe the hunger for honest talk could help all of them.

Jonathan also discussed the special questions that parents have about the lovers of their gay children. His conclusion at the end of the quote is a good one for answering the questions that parents bring up.

I know that the subject of lovers heightens tension for parents and brings up all kinds of questions. For example: As parents, how do you talk to the lover your gay child brings home? Do you acknowledge they are lovers? Do you raise the question about who will sleep where? If the lover has children, do you invite them to your home? Do you send them birthday cards? Do you ever talk about, or with, the parents of the lover? Will you meet them? What if there are religious differences? How do you introduce lovers to the relatives? Can you relate to the lover with honest feelings, or are you up-tight because of guilt about gayness? How do you react to conflicts in the relationship? Or breakups? Or the introduction of a new lover?

All in all, it's a tough ball game. It comes down to one thing though. If parents can see gays as just people, and gays can see parents as people, then we can work together on all these questions—like any adults who care about one another.

RESULTS OF SHARING

While many of our parents chose to share the fact of their child's homosexuality with the rest of the family, some others did not. We do not recommend that everyone necessarily can or should tell other members of the family. In thinking about all of the stories we heard, we came to the conclusion that parents did best when they listened to their own hearts. When the time and circumstances felt reasonably comfortable, the parents let the others know.

Those who did were pleased with the results. There often was created a feeling of family security that gave support to all its members. It was a support that was strong and unyielding to outside pressure. As the gay member received honest acceptance, each family member felt he or she was accepted too.

I feel closer to everyone I've told in the family. I also notice they are willing to tell me about their own concerns. The whole family seems more honest and aware of each other's needs. We're more like good friends. To the question "How are you?" I hear more real answers than "Just fine."

■

I should have had enough sense to realize that no family fits the "perfect" image. It's not necessary to get your self-esteem from that sort of thing.

Because my son turned out to be gay, I was forced to give up that hurtful idea of conforming to a fake image. I'm glad I was forced to do it because it helped me get more in touch with myself and with all my children. I think it even had a good effect on my marriage. To some extent we had been living an illusion, and now that is gone.

Having a gay person in the family has strengthened all of us. For a few months we tottered a bit. In fact, it was very rocky. We know now that we will give each other support for the rest of our lives. Oh, sometimes we are critical and irritable and have family blowups, but when the smoke dies down we come back together again.

*The way you feel and act now
about your child's gayness is
not the way you will feel and
act next year.*

■

E I G H T

■

LEVELS OF
UNDERSTANDING

arents went through stages as they progressed in their journey of understanding, acceptance, and beyond. We call these stages "levels of understanding." At each level, parents focused on different aspects of the issue—first on themselves, then on their gay or lesbian child, and finally on gays and lesbians everywhere.

In the beginning, parents have a need to get control of their feelings while maintaining contact with their gay child. We describe this focus as "Level I Understanding." When parents are at this level, they direct their actions and attentions primarily toward themselves. Easing their own inner conflict is their prime goal.

As the work continues, there is a gradual change of emphasis. After finding comfort and getting accurate information, the parents begin to reach out to their gay child. They want to understand their child's needs, problems, and strengths. Their own needs take a backseat. When this occurs, parents have moved to "Level II Understanding."

Once parents take care of themselves and recognize where their child fits into the scheme of things, they are ready for another move. They begin to broaden their concern to include the welfare of all gay people. This signals that parents have reached "Level III Understanding."

These levels are a somewhat predictable educational pattern as parents learn not only to accept but also to appreciate their child's gayness. Getting all kinds of facts, changing their inner perceptions, and telling others enables parents to move through their levels of understanding. The whole process is like the educational system where children advance from primary to secondary and then to higher levels by learning history, math, and reading throughout their school years.

Not all the parents interviewed went through all levels because they entered the situation from a variety of backgrounds and circumstances. Overall, their movement through the levels was a long-term process. Some parents who previously had known gay or lesbian people moved faster. Also, involvement with a parents of lesbians and gays group early in the understanding process helped speed it along.

Another important factor for faster learning was the support that gay and lesbian children gave these parents during their time of confusion. The children answered questions about themselves and their private lives, reassured parents about cause, presented an assured manner, and understood their parents' feelings. Sometimes it was hard for the children to hear their parents express homophobic fears and concerns. But their patience was rewarded. Over and over, parents also expressed appreciation for the understanding, education, and care their children provided.

All parents interviewed became aware of a reciprocal gain that developed as each level evolved. One mother summed it up when she said, "As we worked to understand and accept our children, we learned a lot about understanding and accepting ourselves." Let us examine more closely the three levels of understanding, as experienced and described by our parents.

LEVEL I: SELF-CENTERED CONCERN

At this level, parents were concerned primarily with their own grief, and rightly so. They were reacting to an all-encompassing sense of loss. As with all major losses, parents at Level I had to mourn. Their self-centeredness at this period sometimes caused parents to feel ashamed and their gay or lesbian child to feel impatient. But mourning is a tough experience, and this self-concern is the necessary first step toward seeing the issue in a new light.

Parents were gripped by society's negative view, and homosexuality was thought to be abnormal. Yet, they often longed that somehow society could be different. There was little communication with anyone, even spouses. Marital relationships were strained. However, within a few days most mothers communicated with a close friend. Fathers usually did not even do that, perhaps because they had been taught to handle crises alone. Opposite sex parents of gay children sometimes had a sense of rejection. Same sex parents often felt they failed to provide the proper role modeling. Overall, parents pretty much isolated themselves, although the lucky ones found a parents' group and attended a meeting.

As for facts, parents started at ground zero. Most of their information was inaccurate. Many were too embarrassed even to get information from the local libraries or bookstores.

In the beginning they rarely took a stand on gayness. Instead, they felt at the mercy of the prevailing misinformation. Jokes and prejudicial comments caused severe anxiety. Fear, for themselves as well as for their gay or lesbian child, was a constant companion. There was a period of paranoia when parents felt they too would be ostracized. Religious attacks against homosexuality were terrifying to them.

Getting beyond Level I took the greatest effort, since they were

emotionally weak, their information was inaccurate, and their isolation was great. But there was intense conflict between what society said about their gay child and what they instinctively knew
about this same child. The pain of the conflict motivated parents
to make new moves. They became open to helpful information
and ignored biased opinions. They expressed a deep commitment toward continuing a mutually satisfying relationship with
their child. With time and effort they graduated to the next
level.

LEVEL II: CHILD-CENTERED CONCERN

Adjusting parents slowly found they were concentrating more and
more of their concern on their child. They were surprised to find
themselves operating at this level. Negative feelings were not as intense. Even though parents had "blue" days, the setbacks were temporary. When being completely honest, parents still wished their
child were not gay, and they still had some trouble with the sexual aspects. But what was of more concern for them were the problems society imposed on that child.

Because parents were less self-centered, they were now willing
to reach out and help other parents. Many attended meetings of
gays and lesbians and shared their stories in the hope of helping
other young people who were deciding to come out.

At this point, parents told us the relationship with their own
child was getting better. Usually these children also reported a
sense of relief at seeing their parents improve. Their worst fears
of being rejected had not materialized, and they often felt they
were back in the family circle. Parents became deeply aware of how
difficult it had been for their gay or lesbian child and their main
goal was to provide a haven for the child.

Parents now pursued the facts with zeal. They learned to read
carefully and to examine the source of both positive and negative
statements. They discovered that the negative view was usually
prejudicial opinion, whereas a positive outlook was more likely to

come from accurate information. Parents became convinced that society was far too harsh on the gay and lesbian community.

Most parents had come out to their close friends, but few had told grandparents and other extended family members. There were times when some would stand up publicly. They would speak for gay rights in the media if they could be anonymous. In general, the parental message was "I have a gay child and it is okay with me—just don't let them know my last name." The more exposure that parents had to standing up for their children, the more likely they were to move to the last level of understanding.

LEVEL III: CONCERN FOR ALL GAYS AND LESBIANS AND THEIR PARENTS

At this level, the parents had no doubt that an injustice had been perpetrated on gays and lesbians. The parents analyzed their own situation and abilities, and within that framework took some action.

Their struggle helped them feel stronger, both individually and as a group. In the absence of any role model these parents had to create new values and guideposts based on the reality of having gay children. It was a frightening place to be, but it was powerful and sometimes exhilarating.

Parents now saw real benefits from the situation. They no longer thought the lives of their gay and lesbian children should be carbon copies of their own, and they related to their gay children as they did to their nongay children. They found satisfaction from friendships with other gay and lesbian people. If they were in self-help groups, they had formed close friendships that they valued highly.

Now, sure of their facts, they were not threatened by different opinions. They regularly looked for opportunities to inform the misinformed. From this point on, parents committed themselves to standing against the prevailing negative view. Their stand was incorporated into the fabric of their lives. They did not allow jokes or disparaging remarks to go unchallenged. They were not afraid of criticism. A few even went on television with their story and their facts. Often they were more out than the children, since they would suffer no legal discrimination.

Two of the parents we interviewed illustrate clearly this movement through the levels. Helen gives a wide variety of details, while Jack describes fully how his inner perception changed.

HELEN'S STORY*

Helen is a white, middle-class schoolteacher who has been married for twenty-eight years to the same man. Both parents have devoted time and energy to their three children and enjoyed it. It is the oldest son who is gay.

Our son came out to us when he was seventeen years old. I remember that he said, "Mom and Dad, I'm gay. You've always thought you've known a lot about me, and you do. Now you know one thing more. It's important to me that you know all about my life and that you be able to share it with me." I had a numb feeling. It was a shock. I didn't want to have heard it. John and Craig began talking, and John was upset. Craig was calm. I didn't say much.

We went to my sister's as soon as we got dressed. She helped us because she accepts gayness as a natural way of life. While we were there, John got down on his knees and begged Craig not to act on his homosexuality. I remember John saying, "If you really are a homosexual it will be okay, but you don't know for sure. You're too young." But, in fact, everyone knew there was no question about Craig's being gay.

During this time I was not involved. I just watched everything that was going on. John and my sister and Craig were interacting, but I was not. Later on that day I saw a boy and girl walking in the park holding hands. I knew Craig would never do that. My eyes teared up, and a heavy feeling settled on my chest. That feeling stayed with me for a long time.

*This is the mother's version of finding out that was told by the father at the opening of Chapter One.

Helen made an early and crucial decision to accept her son's homosexuality as an undeniable fact. Then she began to change herself by examining her feelings and belief system in detail. This is an important decision that allows parents not to waste time on futile dreams.

I was very self-centered. I did not deal with my son. I don't like saying that. I would like to think that I was kind and understanding as I reached out toward Craig, but I wasn't. I was hurting, and I didn't understand why it hurt so much. I didn't think about Craig for a good while. In fact, it was some time before I realized what a traumatic experience he had gone through.

I was ashamed, and that was a first for me concerning my children. There was little help. I told my sister and one friend, and that was it. I thought we were the only couple on the face of the earth that ever had a gay child.

I used to sit and listen to gay jokes and cringe, but I said nothing. More than once I had to leave a room to keep from crying. I gained a lot of weight and felt very depressed. I was lonely.

Parents often fear for themselves as well as for their children. They see themselves facing the same kind of rejection their gay children have had to face.

Because I'm a teacher, I was afraid that if the people in the town found out about my son, I would have a lot of problems with my job. I even thought I might get fired. At the time I definitely felt I had caused Craig's homosexuality. So it made sense to me that it was not the homosexual who should be fired, but the parent.

Helen found herself monitoring the most common actions. This was an unsettling experience.

One of the biggest problems we had with our son's homosexuality had to do with rules. All the little social rules that we knew so well didn't seem to fit. There were no guideposts. We didn't know how to react to him and his lover. We questioned how we would all act around his grandparents. We were in trouble, but we didn't know where to turn. For a while we had no idea even how to talk about Craig. General conversations with our family and friends became a chore.

Parental concern for their own sexuality is very common, and for some it creates a sense of insecurity. It may be the prime reason for extremely negative reactions.

After I found out that Craig was gay, I thought about sexuality a lot. And I worried about mine. I never really had any doubts about my heterosexuality, but there was a little part of me that was afraid. When I was in school, there was a term called "latent homosexuality." My understanding of this term was that a person could be sitting on an unknown time bomb that could go off if just the right set of circumstances came about. And there wouldn't be any inkling that you were gay unless those circumstances happened. I remember thinking, "I have good women friends. Does that mean I could be gay?" Now I realize what a silly and homophobic thought that was.

The search for cause motivated by her guilt occupied much of Helen's thoughts for some time.

When Craig came out to us, I thought that homosexuality was a mental problem of some kind. So his being gay was a crushing blow—a gut-level failure. I thought, "What am I here for if I did this to my baby?" I didn't know how, I didn't know when, I didn't know what I had done. I searched through his growing-up years, but nothing seemed to fit what I'd read.

Still, the finger of guilt pointed straight at me. I have trouble finding the words to say how bad I felt. But I wanted someone to take away my pain. I wanted someone to ease my burden of guilt.

After a while, I began to cope a little. I found out some information and began to see things more realistically. Although I began to feel better, the low times still came. For a long time I had more bad days than good. I'd have to catch hold of myself and fight the old fears repeatedly.

I have always been in a series of roles. I've been a daughter, wife, mother, teacher. Without one of these roles to give me support I didn't know how to act. It was important for me to be successful in all of them. When I found out my son was gay, a funny thing happened. Not only was my mothering role tested and found wanting, but so was my role as a wife.

On top of thinking I had failed my son, I felt like I had failed John because his son was not the all-American boy. I needed John to reassure me about this and to convince me I wasn't a failure to him and the rest of the family.

He couldn't do that. At that time he wanted me to assure him that he wasn't a failure as a father. Neither of us could make the pain go away for the other.

Ideally we should have been leaning on one another and giving support. In truth we didn't give each other any help at all. I wanted to be a little girl and be petted, and understood and allowed to cry. But he couldn't let me do that because he was suffering the same way I was.

For some time I was withdrawn from John and he was from me. It was as if we each went off into a shell somewhere. Neither of us could understand why we were so hurt. We couldn't understand why we were so fearful, and we felt bad about feeling that way.

Just before Craig told us, I can remember thinking, "We're like one of those ideal TV families. We have one girl and two boys. They're all on the honor roll at school. John and I have a good relationship. Life just can't be better. We did it. We've done a good job." For a while it looked like our world was full of roses. But after we found out that Craig was gay, all the roses wilted.

Everyone in the family had a hard time. We went from having a perfect family image to being just a bunch of individuals who peeped out at each other and said, "Why don't you make it better for me?" None of us was able to do that. We all wanted to, but everyone was too weak. We were not a good support system at that time.

This mother next reported actions which started her movement from a self-centered stage to an understanding of her son's position.

For a good while I wondered if my grief would ever be completely over. I suffered the death of a dream. A part of it was being a good mother according to what my neighbors would think. I wanted to be accepted and looked up to by society. But there was more to this grief than that. I've had trouble figuring out what it was all about.

I got some help. I talked to a counselor. It was good just to talk it through. But you have to be careful whom you talk to. You want someone who understands homosexuality and accepts it as a positive way of life.

Craig helped us right after he told us; also later on as we began to understand what had happened. He was able to reassure us on almost everything that we were afraid of.

He constantly forced us to face up to the fact that he was gay. He insisted on being the person he was. He started pressing early to bring his boyfriend home. We didn't want him to, but Craig brought him home anyway. We liked him and we liked the way they acted toward each other. Seeing their mutual care and concern eased our fear that Craig would always be lonely.

Now as I think back over it, I am filled with a feeling of being loved by Craig. It must have been hard for him to see his parents react as negatively as we did. But his self-confidence made us both feel better. It still does.

When I think of how it was for him, I feel sad. Craig first discovered he was gay when he was thirteen. He said that at night he would lie in bed and cry because he knew what he was, and he could not change it. He got lonelier and lonelier. He tried to do everything really well, and he received honors throughout high school. But his loneliness would not go away. He's a very attractive kid, and a lot of girls were after him. He saw girls during that whole time, trying to cover up, trying to get interested in a female. But he couldn't. I wish John and I could have helped him more.

Having worked through some of her early grieving, this mother made another decision that is typical of parents in the middle level of understanding. She decided to take a risk and tell someone else about her situation. This led to the major source of help for her—other parents.

I was taking a class on sexism in education at a local college. Following one of our class discussions, the teacher asked if we would like to learn something about homosexuality. Most people in the room agreed that they would.

After class, when the professor was alone in front of the room, I got up enough courage to tell her about Craig. There were tears in my eyes as I talked. She didn't say anything, just reached over and took my hand. I still remember the feel of her hand on mine. She looked gently at me. She understood. I didn't have to tell her anything else. It was a beautiful moment.

Soon after, a gay man came to talk to our class. He was sure of himself and seemed very well put together as a person. Most of all, he was proud of himself. Meeting him made me feel better. I guess that was the first time I began to see homosexuality as just another way of living. He made it okay for me.

Later he took John and me over to a parents' group meeting. I sat and cried. The people there understood. John talked too, and we were not alone. We became just two of many who were fighting for our children.

In general, each time a parent chooses to tell someone about having a gay son or lesbian daughter, the chains of prejudice are loosened.

Telling is a big decision for parents. It certainly was for me. John and I had a big disagreement over telling his folks. We never did, and I don't feel as close to them. I felt forced to choose between them and my child, and I resented it.

Every time I told someone about Craig's being gay, I felt stronger. I'm not sure why. Maybe it was because I was in control, and I was supporting Craig.

Helen's son has moved back into his accustomed role in family situations, and Helen has now reached Level III. She accepts her gay son, her parenting, and other gays and lesbians.

Now Craig can tell us pretty much anything he wants to. He expects us to love him, no matter what. And that's an expectation we've met. He's our son, and we love him just like he is.

I worry about him the way I worry about my other two children. I think he is very courageous and strong as a gay person in this society. He doesn't let prejudicial statements get him down. If he does have problems, he feels he can handle them. I think he can. He doesn't make the situation worse than it is.

You know, a funny thing happened about this idea of love. All of our children say that we love them more than parents usually love their children. I think it's because we were tested, and we passed. Our children have no doubts that we will accept them for what they are.

When I look back over my progress since I found out that Craig was gay, I realize that I expected myself to be too accepting too soon. I didn't give myself the right to have bad feelings. I condemned them instead. My basic feelings for Craig are caring, love, and concern. I have felt those since he was born. They will not change. I would have been better off had I just given myself the right to explore my negative feelings.

Now I think that John and I are good parents. We provided a good climate for our children to grow up in.

A few months ago our parents' group met with a group of gay teenage boys. As I sat and listened to their sad stories of loneliness and rejection, I felt ashamed. I thought, "I was a part of hurting these youngsters when I believed it was wrong to be gay. I kept quiet when I heard derogatory remarks. These boys don't deserve this." That evening I moved all the way over. All my prejudice went away. Now I think of those children as being my children, and I'm going to do everything I can to help make this a better place for them.

Lately I've even told some parents of the students I teach in school. I will appear on TV or on radio if I'm asked. I'm not too worried about what other people think, and I feel stronger and more sure of myself. I am proud of the way John and I have handled the whole situation.

I've had to face a mountain of prejudice against homosexuality. Some of it was inside me and some of it was out there in the town where I live. The climb has given me a hardy sense of worthiness. I've begun to look at all my thinking more carefully. I feel more in charge of my life.

The mountain hasn't been totally climbed. I suspect it never will be. When I think I'm at the top, another hill appears and I have to go over that. But I'm not afraid of those hills. They're small in comparison to the enormous mountain that I've already conquered.

JACK'S STORY*

Jack is a sixty-three-year-old professor at a prestigious university in the Midwest. He has known about his son's gayness for nine years. He and his wife, who have three children, helped form a parents' group in their town. Chris, their middle child and only son, is gay.

When Chris decided to tell his parents about his gayness, he tried to find ways to ease the sense of loss that he expected them to feel. He had thoughtfully provided counseling help for the family, and this got them started on the right foot. Though Jack's initial reaction was mild, he quickly saw the need to face his negative feelings honestly and openly. This action is a lot easier to say than do. Few of us want to admit that we have trouble accepting something basic about our children.

In the next few quotes Jack clearly describes the beginning level of understanding. He was primarily concerned with himself and his feelings.

I remember when Chris told us he was gay. We were stunned, and for a time his announcement was followed by silence. Then he started to cry. I just went over and put my arms around him.

I was shaken by it. I had a lot of mixed feelings. Chris was in training as a clinical psychologist, and he had talked with a therapist about the possibility of our coming to see him. The whole family went the next day. That was a big help. We got feelings out. Part of me was kind of numb. I hadn't really accepted it, but having a chance to talk it out was a lucky break. It was a useful thing for that immediate occasion, but it didn't get me around the corner in terms of really accepting homosexuality.

Fairly soon we flew back home, and got in touch with the local gay church to find out if there was a parents' group. There wasn't, but we were invited to attend one of their services.

The church service really shook me. I had trouble fighting back the tears

*This is the father's version of finding out described earlier by the mother in Chapter One.

during the service. There were gay and lesbian couples going up to the altar together holding hands. I wasn't feeling positive about that. I was thinking, "Is Chris going to be into something like this?" I was feeling sorry for myself that that would happen. But I had all sorts of mixed feelings, because I also thought there were very tender feelings between these people.

Then when they were singing hymns like the ones in the Methodist Church I grew up in, I began having flashbacks. I wondered how my mother would have experienced this. It was a Christian service, but with something "peculiar" going on. I don't think she could have handled it. I was having strong feelings during the service, fighting back tears the whole time.

As is typical with many fathers of gay sons, Jack remembers trying to develop a father-son relationship with the usual male pursuits.

I had had bad feelings about our relationship when Chris was growing up. I felt a failure. I couldn't seem to make contact with him. He seemed irritated with me a lot, and I'd get irritated with him.

I kept trying to get Chris into playing catch, and he just wasn't interested. So I thought, "Okay, don't lay my trip on him. Let him be where he is."

Later I then tried to get him interested in Boy Scouts. He had no interest in that either. I don't think we went to more than three or four meetings.

The scouts had a father-and-son overnight that fall. We were in pup tents, and there was an early snow. Chris got sick and had to be taken home during the night. It just seemed like nothing was working.

In the next quote we are given a good example of a parent who is moving into the middle level of understanding (the child-centered stage). He is very aware of the needs of his son and of his own needs.

For a while after finding out, Marilyn and I had a tendency not to talk about it. It was easier to talk about anything else. Finally, we agreed that the subject would be one we would actively bring up. We began to move.

When Chris came home the first time after telling us, he probed about where we were in our understanding. He wanted us to assure him that we totally accepted his homosexuality. We both said we couldn't—that we hadn't made our peace with it yet. We didn't give him anything phony. He had to accept us where we were.

That was one of the first corners we got around. It was a critical step for all of us to stay with reality. Being exactly where we were was the most caring thing we could do. He had been honest with us when he came out, and that set the tone for how we had to deal with each other.

At some point I decided that I had to make some kind of adjustment about his gayness. I could not become fixated on my own misery and discomfort. I had to let go of it. I didn't like it, but gradually I decided it was his life.

I've moved to the point where I can deal honestly with Chris. We can be open about one of the heaviest of issues, homosexuality. It's a number one challenge, because I started as far back as anyone.

All the ideas I had of homosexuality were negative. It was something I don't remember ever talking about. My image was that gays were people who picked up sex in the park. It was dirty and was done by people with strange mannerisms. Then I realized that I, myself, was now associated with gayness. My child was into something that repels a lot of people. I'm now part of it.

So my feelings about homosexuality in general were riding heavily on my shoulders. They were wrapped around me, and I had trouble getting them off.

Rather than continuing to put himself down for not being perfect in this whole process, Jack accepts himself where he is.

Perfectionism is a tyranny that I've had trouble shaking. I thought I had to give up all my negative feelings in order to have a good relationship with Chris. But anger and negative feelings are just a part of living. There's always ambivalence. Right now, I say I'll probably always have wishes that he weren't a homosexual. He's without a partner, and I often think he will have a lonely kind of battle.

While I still have my hang-ups about homosexuality, I know we also have moved closer to each other. I feel good that Chris and I can hug each other. He now says he wants us to live near him in California. When I think about

*how much of a failure I felt in relation to Chris when he was growing up,
I find these changes remarkable.*

If Jack had stopped here, he and Chris would probably be reasonably comfortable together. But he made a deliberate choice to continue working. A year later Jack reported further movement in his relations with Chris.

Significant changes have continued to take place. Until about a year ago I harbored many regrets. I still thought if I had a choice, I would want Chris to be heterosexual. Even after all my involvement in the parents' group, I joined the long line of parents who said, "Of course we wouldn't choose it for our child."

I've gotten away from that, and I'm trying to get in touch with why. I think it has to do with what has happened and with a change of perception about what really has been good for my life and for Chris. But the changes came only after some hard discussions with him.

One summer evening around the fire at our mountain cabin in Colorado, I told Chris of my continuing distaste for the sexual acts between men.

He was hurt that I would come back with statements and feelings out of the old places. It was hard for him to hear me go back to these harsh messages. But he knew they were in me, and he was willing to face the issues once again.

In these tough confrontations with Chris I got into the real nitty-gritty. I can't recount all the details, but as we talked, I heard myself realizing truths about sex that I had pushed aside. Chris pointed out that nongays engage in the same sexual behaviors which are condemned for gays, and that therefore the image of "dirty" that I had associated with gay sex was also valid for heterosexual sex.

I became aware that I had resisted acknowledging these facts. I have mixed feelings about the whole sexual revolution. Deeply rooted within me is the traditional western teaching that only heterosexual sex is okay. But I also know that I welcome for myself a wider range of sexual expression, including what I was condemning in gay people. I began to realize how hypocritical I was being. I finally could laugh at myself.

Jack then expressed feelings that come to parents who have moved beyond acceptance. It is a level that has its own reward.

I have come to realize that my son's being gay has been a major source of personal liberation for me. I grew up in a conservative, German neighborhood with the message: "Keep in mind what the neighbors will think." I have gradually come to realize how crippling and burdensome that message is. It asked me not to look at the world through my own eyes and not to face the truth about my life as I experienced it. I spent too much of my energy trying to keep up appearances.

If Chris had not been gay, I would have let life cheat me. In a very real sense he rescued me from that. I am freer now to take other risks as I face what I want to do with my life.

It is Chris's nature to be gay. That is the way he came into the world, and the way he is in the world. I would never change him even if I could. He and all the other gay and lesbian children have a right to be here as they are. They can help us expand our lives by widening the range of differences that we can embrace and enjoy.

Learning to appreciate being parents of lesbian and gay children is a process, not an end point. Our society continually changes, and adjusted parents have the capacity and self-confidence to grow and change as the need arises.

NINE

CONTRAST AND COMPARISON OF WHAT WAS AND WHAT WILL BE

I *have a fantasy about America in twenty more years. I'll be eighty then. I'll be this little old lady who, back in the 1980s worked for gay people's rights. Instead of saying, "You were brave," I hope they'll say, "Gay rights? You mean they haven't always had rights? Are you sure you're not making this up?" I look forward to the time when the parents' organization will be out of business, no longer needed.*

■

When I look at him, I sometimes want to cry because I'm so proud of the way he handled it when everyone in the world told him he wasn't okay. I can hardly believe one of my children had that much courage, awareness, ability, self-confidence, to know he was okay. Even when we were doubtful, he didn't lash back at us. He just went on.

It has been a hard struggle. But finally we have come to see gayness as a gift instead of a curse.

IMAGES OF THE FUTURE

The following quotations present a direct picture of the future that parents want to come about. They are good examples of what "beyond acceptance" really means.

Some day homosexuality will be taken as much for granted as heterosexuality. People will not only accept gay rights as ordinary, they'll say, "Why did it take us so long to come to our senses?"

■

When we parents speak publicly, the audiences are frozen with interest. There is no sound, no movement. I hope someday that will change, that people will be bored with it all and say, "What was all the fuss about? Of course some people are gay. What of it?"

■

It is my hope that in challenging the lies, myths, and gossip about gay people, we'll create a new generation of parents. These parents will have such accurate information about homosexuality that they won't see it as an unusual or threatening thing if one or more of their children turns out to be gay. It will be more like having a curly-haired child or a straight-haired one, a tall one or a short one.

■

To me homosexuality is not a matter of right and wrong. It's just a part of the way things are. We all have our daily way of life. We're not used to all the new things we've been learning the past few years. But because of

TV, radio, and other media, we hear more about different ways of life than we ever have in the past.

I think that within fifteen or twenty years this whole issue about homosexuality will be a dead issue. Our society has gone through this with all different ethnic groups as they came into the country. When I was a child, Jewish people were considered strange exotic people in my neighborhood. Blacks were the same. Catholics were suspect. Even left-handed people were looked down on. Every kind of person who is different, unfortunately, has had to go through this. Now the gay people are going through it. But I have no doubt that they will come out on the other side if we keep working and educating and raising people's awareness.

The next generation of parents should have much better information and preparation for dealing with a gay child. I don't want other families to have to suffer and struggle to get information like we did.

CHANGES IN PARENTAL ATTITUDES

When parents are helped to escape from their closet, perhaps one toe at a time, they enter a world of new possibilities—a new perception of the world. It is one that is exciting and satisfying. The following statements show this before and after change:

What parents said at first: *Don't tell a soul. Cover it up. Lie if necessary.*

What they said later: *How can I ask anyone to deny the basic sexual orientation of his or her life? How would I like to be made to feel ashamed of my heterosexuality? If other people condemn, it's because they know nothing about the facts.*

■

At first: *Why should we change? We're not the ones with the problem.*

Later: *I realize now I did have a problem. I thought my way was the only way to be. I found that prejudice, though hard to give up, was an enormous burden.*

■

At first: *Don't make us question our religion.*

Later: *My religion means even more to me now, and presents no conflict. I realized the real message of all religions is to love, not judge, those who are different from me.*

■

At first: *Above all, don't show your affection for your lover in front of us or the relatives.*

Later: *You have a right to express affection the same as our straight children, no more, no less. The family customs of "good taste" should operate on a single standard.*

■

At first: *If you must be gay, then try to be perfect in every other way, to compensate.*

Later: *You can be yourself, imperfect like the rest of us. Strong in some areas, not so strong in others. We love you as you are. If we have gripes, we'll talk them out the same as we would with any other loved one.*

■

At first: *How could you do this to me? Do you realize the pain this is causing?*

Later: *My pain forced me to face the conflict between myths I'd been taught and scientific facts about homosexuality. Some of the pain stems from my own resistance to change. Accepting differences in others helps me to be kinder to myself, to accept my own differences.*

■

At first: *I can't bear to risk the rejection of my relatives, friends, or neighbors by admitting I have a gay child.*

Later: *I found that the relatives, friends, and neighbors that I care about like me more when I can follow my own conscience and not be dependent on their opinions.*

CHANGES IN PARENTS' PERCEPTIONS OF GAYNESS

The fundamental changes that took place in the lives of accepting parents were reflected in their everyday language. We now listen to them describe, with personal detail, their new way of perceiving the world of their gay children.

Society says our gay children are disturbed, weak, and immoral. I find them to be mature, of high principles, and persistently of strong character. Others say gay people are ridiculous or outrageous. I find them to be loving, sensitive, both serious and humorous. "They" call them failures. I find successes. Gays and lesbians are called unmanly or unwomanly. I find them deep, fully developed men and women.

■

I don't want her to be alone. I'm glad she found someone. It's her life. If she's happy, that's the important thing.

■

Everyone doesn't live like you do, or like I do. Everyone has a different way. There are so many different lifestyles. Being gay is just one more of them. I don't approve of it for me, but that doesn't mean it's wrong.

■

One friend asked me, "Wouldn't you like it better if he wasn't gay?" And I can very honestly say no. It doesn't matter a bit. Paul is Paul. Once I got past the stage of thinking of all the terrible things that crazy people with guns might do to him . . . when I got past that, I no longer cared that he was gay. If he were somebody else . . . if he were straight, maybe he'd be different. And I don't want him different in any way. This is him. Being gay is part of him. He's a wonderful young man. Now I confess, I do wish he'd stand up straight. He's going to have a bad back by the time he's thirty.

■

I feel very good toward Ken. It never crosses my mind that he might change some day, or wouldn't it be nice if he were to change. I really don't

*care about that. That's a dead issue. We get along very well. Of course,
he lives a distance away which makes it easier to get along, because we're
not involved in any nitty-gritty daily problems. But still, when we're together, we're immediately in tune with one another. It's a good feeling.
And I see his lifestyle as perfectly okay. I still think it's inconvenient in
our society, but that's not his fault. I don't think he's done anything
wrong. I regret, to put it mildly, that our society penalizes gays and their
families.*

WHY GAY PEOPLE WANT TO COME OUT TO PARENTS

As gay people gain self-pride, they get tired and impatient with having to maintain old deceptions. They don't want to be treated better than their heterosexual brothers and sisters. They simply want
to be accepted as they were accepted when they were children—
as human beings who have the same right to be here with their
special uniqueness as any other person on earth. That's another
reason for their deep need to tell parents—"to find out if I'm loved
for who I really am." The following quotations, one from a gay man
and one from a lesbian, poignantly convey their need to come out
to their families:

*In growing up, I had experienced life about like other kids. Some prob-
lems, of course, but in general I was just another part of the family, of school
life, and of the rest of the world. When I gradually discovered I wasn't like
my peers, that I might be gay, all of this that I had been able to take for
granted began to change.*

*In many ways, I felt less than a whole person, even though I hadn't
shared my feelings with a single soul. I was now one of those "terrible people." I took in the feeling that there was something dreadfully wrong with
me—something so awful that if it was discovered, I might lose the parental
love I was so dependent on for a good part of my existence. Or, because of
this deeply awful thing about myself, I might be a source of great hurt to
my parents. I longed to tell them and to be told I was loved, no matter what.*

■

After my sister had put her children to bed, I sat down with her and after a few minutes finally blurted out, "Sherry, what I wanted to tell you is that I'm gay." She replied, "Well, okay" and took the news in a calm manner.

Then she said she had a question to ask me, and said, "I don't think it's any of my affair what your sexual life is like. I don't talk about my sexual life to anybody, and I don't see why you need to even worry about whether to tell us or not. What is all this business about gay people wanting to come out of the closet? Why tell people what you're doing? Why on earth would you people want to talk about it?"

I explained that it's because of the prejudice against us. We feel that we cannot be openly seen to be affectionate with a member of the same sex. We fear loss of our jobs or status or friendships. Whereas if you're married, you're openly with your beloved all the time. And that's the way it's "supposed to be." When you're heterosexual, you don't have to talk about your sex life because your sexuality is understood and affirmed automatically.

I also spoke about my sense of alienation from the family gatherings when everyone was together with their spouses and their families. The family gatherings were the worst times for me, because I had someone that I loved too, but I felt I couldn't say, "Let me bring my partner. She's the one I really care about." So I felt I was the loner in the family.

WHY PARENTS NEED THEIR CHILDREN TO COME OUT TO THEM

When children are honest with their parents about being lesbian or gay, they risk a great deal. So those who tell their parents show strength of character and real love for them. They want the relationship to be marked by complete integrity. To have that, they must be out of the closet and up front about the reality of their lives. Without this kind of sharing, the individuals are like actors performing prescribed roles. They are not present to each other as the real persons they are.

Children come to their parents with trust as well as fear. They are telling themselves, "Even if my parents may not approve, they will be there for me. They will still love me, they will respect my sincerity, and they will take my comments seriously." That trust is a great compliment to a parent. It implies that a truly loving parent-child relationship exists. There is communication, love, caring, honesty, and a desire to let everyone in the relationship be who they are.

With trust present, even if approval is delayed, gay and lesbian people tend to be able to cope with any problem. So do the other family members. This doesn't mean they breeze through life easily. They have just as many serious problems as anyone else. But when confronted with a difficult situation, the family members search, bend, persist with all their strength until there is some resolution that is satisfactory to all.

· As parents look back, they realize they've made a connection in the deepest sense with their child. Listen as parents share this awareness.

It takes a lot of courage for our children to tell us. Particularly if they're close to us. That might seem to be a contradiction. But I think it's hard even for those who've had easy, good relationships with their parents, because they don't want to jeopardize that. And they don't want to hurt us. They think and hope we'll accept it. But they're not positive. I think it's important to realize that it's very special, their coming out to us. It's interesting that all the parents I know are not sorry their children told them, though they may have been at first. Even though some of them went through hell, they still prefer to know.

■

I know it was difficult for Mary to tell us; perhaps the most difficult thing she's ever had to do. She told us because she cares so much for us. She felt she had to tell us and I think she wanted to tell us. She wanted us to share in her happiness. I couldn't do that when she first told us, but I can now.

■

Now that she's out in the open, she seems to feel good about herself. Her health is much better, and she's much more open in all her dealings and relationships, both inside and outside the family.

■

Young people who share their homosexuality with their families are not likely to enter into a marriage hoping it will make them heterosexual. They won't make themselves and someone else unhappy. I had a woman friend who was married six years to a man who was gay. She was utterly miserable. I'm sure he was too. She held some hope all those years, and even after she divorced him, that he could change. This kind of thing should not happen. And it probably won't happen if gay people have the love and support of their parents.

■

Everything that's important in your life that you share with someone you care about, intensifies your relationship. So it's made us closer even though we were close before. But if my daughter hadn't told me, and felt that she had to go her way on this, and I go mine, it would have been a barrier. Instead, knowing and sharing this has enriched our relationship. It also opens up a channel for other talk in the future. If we can share this kind of thing, then there is very little else she can't tell me. Or that I couldn't tell her.

Parents also want and need something from their gay children, something that may seem paradoxical at first. The parents we interviewed often said: "We wanted her/him to give us time to adjust, to integrate the new information and to get used to a radical shift of thinking. But we also needed to be confronted firmly and gently if we ran away from the truth or if we were stalling or were misinformed. So we told our gay child: 'Be firm in your belief in yourself and in the honorableness of homosexuality. Tell us you love us, and that you want an open, honest relationship that continues indefinitely.' "

This can be summed up by one father's comment:

She had her life together and was happy. She was proud of being a gay person. Because she accepted herself, it helped give us courage to accept her and ourselves as being just fine the way we are.

GAY PEOPLE, PARENTS, AND SOCIETY

Our gay and lesbian children made clear beyond a doubt that parental support enriched their lives and helped them face a hostile world. Their self-acceptance was achieved more quickly and easily with parents' approval.

When parents supported their children, they supported and healed themselves, and built up their own self-esteem and self-confidence. Just as many gay people have insisted on an honest relationship with their parents, we hope that parents will insist on the same kind of honesty with the rest of society.

When society takes the step of dropping its hostility to such a large section of its own members, it will have made a major step toward furthering its own health—because it will have lowered the level of violent and destructive tendencies within itself.

Parents of my generation (age fifty and up) are apt to feel rejected when their child settles on a sexual orientation that is different from their own. I guess a lot of us have problems with accepting and valuing differences. This is not just a parents' problem, it's a cultural problem. That's why we have racism, and anti-Semitism, and strife between peoples. We haven't learned to appreciate deep fundamental differences in a cooperative and friendly way. We see differences as threats to who we are.

The following is a statement from a young gay man who explains how the peace and caring restored within an accepting family can become a miniature representation for society.

We want to be out of the closet so that we can be close to our families. We don't want to waste energy covering up the basic facts of our lives. Also, we want to be out because some of our greatest strengths and talents can only be expressed freely when we are completely ourselves. When we are not out, to our families, to co-workers, to the world, the constraint that goes into hiding and the inner conflict that daily drains our energy spells a real waste of human intelligence, creativity, and sensitivity.

We want to make a better world for all people, but particularly for gay people in future generations. Most gay people I have talked with feel that their coming out is part of the historical moment. We feel this sense of responsibility and urgency to open things up so that those who come after us won't have to suffer as much as we did. Just like those before us in the forties and fifties, the Daughters of Bilitis, for example, or the men of the Mattachine Society, made possible this discussion that we're having now.

There's something about gay liberation and being open about homosexuality that reverberates far beyond the obvious questions of accepting a difference in sexual orientation. When gay people are out of the closet, the world's eyes are opened to a way of expressing human feeling that does not obey the old system in which only heterosexuality is acceptable. Our present system is one that restricts both men and women, whether heterosexual or homosexual. A calm, complete, and honest sex education dealing with all human diversity can help all children, all people. I'm not talking about the ways our society deals with sexuality through suggestive movies or advertising. This I see as pseudo-openness. All sexuality needs to be brought out in the open in a healthy way. A discussion of the true facts about homosexuality can bring heterosexuality into clearer focus. When we come out to our families, we are raising these issues whether or not they are named.

We hope that in the future people will be less frightened and enraged by differences. Violence against gay people is due to fears about persons who are different, and to myths about dangers they represent. We simply want to be complete human beings without being objects of rage. We don't want special treatment, we want equal treatment. We are asking heterosexual people to accept the reality of homosexuality—to accept us simply as human beings, with the usual range of strengths and weaknesses.

An Interview: Mother and Gay Son

The following is a dialogue between a mother and a gay son, age twenty-four. It concerns what he hopes for in their parent-child relationship in the future. He also discusses the coming out process from his perspective seven years later. He tells what he liked and didn't like about the time he came out at age seventeen. The interview concentrates on the son's thoughts, feelings, and opinions. But there is a hidden message in the dialogue—that the mother could hear her son's past pain without being defensive. She showed empathy for his situation, and he showed empathy for hers.

Parent: *As a gay man, what do you expect of parents? Tell me first what you expect your dad and me to do. And then what you hope all parents would do for their children.*

Son: *I hope that you and Dad will just be supportive. And love me. I don't think that's a small thing. Just be my mom and dad—the same as you always have been. I guess that's what I want. I don't necessarily expect you to accept everything or to like everything about the gay lifestyle. But I hope you'll try to understand another person's point of view and accept me as much as you do my brother and sister. That way you'll treat me as an individual.*

Parent: *When you came out to us, what did you expect?*

Son: *I expected you to get upset and then think it was okay.*

Parent: *Is that what happened?*

Son: *The time factor was a little different than what I expected.*

Parent: *It was a lot slower?*

Son: *Yes.*

Parent: *Is there anything you did during the time that your dad and I were having trouble with the process, that you thought was helpful to us?*

Son: *I guess I was firm. I think that was good. I didn't give in. But at the same time, I don't think I was obnoxious. And I tried to be helpful and provide you with information. I tried to convince you that I was actually the same person and that you just knew me a little better now.*

Parent: *When did you realize you were gay, whether you had a word for it or not?*

Son: *I was fairly positive by the time I was in sixth grade, because I had sexual thoughts about men instead of women. The other boys were talking about girls, and I was thinking about boys. When I was growing up, I was different. And I was ridiculed constantly because I was different.*

Parent: *When do you remember feeling that you were different?*

Son: *I'm not sure—six years old, maybe five years old.*

Parent: *And what were you ridiculed about?*

Son: *Not being good in sports, and for being too feminine.*

Parent: *Called "sissy" and such as that?*

Son: *Yes, but you know, I'm sure every child feels special in a lot of ways. You talk to any gay guy, and he will tell you that he always felt different, even if he didn't know he was gay until he was much older. But I wonder if all children might feel different in some way. Almost everyone has trouble with their sexuality in one way or another. Many children might worry a lot and feel there's something wrong with them, including a large number who aren't gay. And certainly a lot of people who are called sissies don't grow up to be gay. But I think perhaps the insecurity is more intense for gay people.*

Parent: *You were seventeen when you came out to us and twelve when you knew for sure. Between the ages of twelve and seventeen, how was it for you?*

Son: *I thought my life was going to be miserable. And I thought I was sick. I was completely horrified by the immensity of my problem, and how isolated I felt. And there was no one I could talk to.*

Parent: *No one at all? Not one person?*

Son: *No one at all. I didn't talk to anyone until after I came out to myself, and I'd started having sex when I was seventeen.*

Parent: *That's about the same time you told us.*

Son: *Yes.*

Parent: *What during those years was helpful to you?*

Son: *I read a lot. I suppose that was the only thing. I didn't read anything that was helpful about being gay. All I did was bury myself in books because it was a way to escape from life. There was nothing at all that was helpful about being gay. Not a single, solitary thing.*

Parent: *What do you think inside you gave you the courage to come out when you did? You were pretty young.*

Son: *Well, I figured I had a choice. I could go on being miserable and dead inside, or I could at least see if there was any possibility for me to have some kind of interest, some excitement or something sexual that I enjoyed out of my life. Perhaps emotional honesty was what I was after. I kept trying to tell myself it was a stage, and so on—the things gay people always tell themselves to avoid the truth. It took a long time for me to really accept it.*

Parent: *What advice would you give to young gay people that might help their lives as they're growing up?*

Son: *Well, stay off the streets. Try to find some kids your own age who are decent and who are gay, if you can. Form some kind of friendship with them. Try not to grow up in a little town.*

Parent: *I've been thinking about Alan, your first lover. He was very helpful to us. I wonder if we hurt him or your other friends in any way.*

Son: *I think you made them feel good.*

Parent: *How?*

Son: *By talking to them and being interested.*

Parent: *Now on the converse side, was there anything that we did that was hurtful when you came out? I don't want you to whitewash it.*

Son: *The thing that comes to mind, and I don't really blame you for it, was that you and Dad were so hung up about my being different from the time I was four years old. It was obvious that you both were disappointed by the whole notion that I might be gay, or at least different from the all-American kind of little boy. While I was still struggling with accepting my-self, those memories magnified the intensity of the doubts and questions I had in my own head. I think this made it a lot worse for me. But I see you and Dad as having changed a lot.*

Parent: *Do you have any idea as to what we did to change?*

Son: *I think you both reexamined the whole notion of sex roles. Those kinds of things.*

Parent: *How do you view your future as a gay man in this society? Do you think you're going to be hurt by it?*

Son: *Probably. But I just think of life as something to be gotten on with. You just try to do the best you can and muddle through. You hope for the best and see how things go.*

Parent: *From the gay people that you know, is it better to stay in the closet or come out of the closet?*

Son: *Come out of the closet. At least then you have the potential of being happy, more satisfied, and feeling that you're fulfilling your destiny and doing what you want to do. You're in charge of your life.*

Parent: *In other words, when you come out, you don't buy other peo-ple's negative view of homosexuality?*

Son: *I didn't say that. A lot of gay people do buy it. They take it out on themselves in a lot of different ways. But I think you at least have a lot more potential for enjoying your life and doing what you want to do if you're out of the closet. I wouldn't ever try to tell other gays to be open like me. That's an individual decision.*

Parent: *But you needed to come out of the closet?*

Son: *Yes. I have to be myself.*

In the story told, we have seen not only how parents changed their attitudes toward homosexuality, but also how they came to see the possibility of a different future.

The exact features of a society free of homophobia cannot be seen clearly at this time. Our story, however, shows that homophobia can be dropped. As gay people and their families get out from under the burden of the old misconceptions, they want a new relationship not only with each other but with society. They want to be who they are without having to hide, to be labeled, or to be the object of scorn or ridicule. Each person who becomes aware that "gay is okay" and stands up for gay rights, in some way changes society.

Because gay people and their parents have changed, we know it is possible for society to change. As we share the images that parents and their gay and lesbian children have of new ways of living, we can get a glimpse of a more just and fair society.

TEN

ABOUT AIDS
by CAROLYN WELCH GRIFFIN

I first heard about AIDS at the Parents FLAG convention in 1982. Two young doctors spoke, and I still remember them saying, "If you want to help your children, you must warn them. There's something out there that we think is sexually transmitted and it's deadly." I felt fear, but I hoped my son was safe and AIDS would not invade our lives. It has. Our son has cared for two life partners: one who died; the other has many opportunistic infections, and Greg himself is approaching full-blown AIDS.

AIDS is a disaster that has been happening to my family for ten years now. We are not alone. There are many thousands of families who are in the same boat. One of my former students has died from the virus; a woman I first met thirty years ago is hiding the fact that her son died from AIDS; my principal in the school district where I worked for twenty-four years was struck down; when I mentioned that my son had AIDS to a department store clerk who lives in my town, she began to cry and said that her son had died from AIDS five years ago and that she had told no one; we have had several families in our Parents FLAG chapter who have lost children or whose children are ill. But within the framework of this illness, I have become increasingly aware of hope, love, and an appreciation of each day.

This disease is one of unwelcomed surprises. It is a roller coaster of hope and despair. As the white T cells are destroyed by the HIV virus, the immune system becomes compromised. The body can then be attacked by any number of toxic agents. Persons affected by this virus have few ways to predict what their future holds. Even the time alloted to live is highly unpredictable. Some people are long-time survivors, while others can move to a deadly disease shortly after becoming infected. On the plus side, the medical community has learned to manage many opportunistic infections. These medical advances, along with psychological support, often allow the quality of life to be quite good for some time.

JOURNAL ENTRIES

In 1982 I was feeling fine about having a gay son. Much had happened to me that had given me more choices for my life than I had ever had. Parents FLAG Saint Louis was going strong; my circle of friends had widened; Rod and I were proud of how our family had handled our homophobia; Greg had a new relationship with Nagib, a young man from the Middle East, that seemed promising. But that strange disease was sitting out there, and no one knew whom it would strike next. I found myself in a low but chronic state of anxiety and fear. I said to Greg, "I'm afraid for you."

"I'm fine," he said. "I've done a statistical analysis of the probability that I could get this disease, and my getting it is very remote. You have nothing to worry about, Mother." At that time he was already infected, though he didn't know it.

By 1983 I had begun keeping a journal as I prepared to become a counselor. It is from these journals that most of the rest of the material in this chapter will come.

The Early Years

July 26, 1984

Greg called last night, excited and happy about his new job at Rockwell. I liked what I heard. I like Greg. I don't like him living in L.A. I wish he were closer.

November 25, 1984

"I'm a big boy," Greg said when he was two. Rod and I laughed and thought he was a brilliant boy. We still do, though now he's a brilliant man.

June 10, 1985

We've been to L.A. to visit with Greg and Nagib. They seem well suited. They're in their new condominium, which we helped them get. It feels good to be as committed to Greg and Nagib's relationship as I am to my other children's. The vacation was one of the best we've had in years. Rod and I rested physically, emotionally, and psychologically.

We needed it. We've been bombarded with frightening information about AIDS. Everything I've read and heard points out how vulnerable Greg and Nagib are. Apparently your body's immune system is impaired as the virus attacks the white cells, which keep you healthy.

September 27, 1985

Nagib's immune system is down. We're almost sure that he and Greg have the disease.

November 11, 1985

We had a talk with Greg. He admitted not practicing safe sex until six months ago. He said that he had had a rash on his leg and that his glands had been swollen. His doctor told him he had had some kind of herpes. As he talked, I could feel his fear die down; Rod's and mine went up.

March 20, 1986

It's closing in on Greg's birthday. Sometimes I think that because we had such a hard time when he came out to us that he may have felt that his parents died for him at that time. Rod wants to put his arms around him, and so do I.

July 1, 1986

Nagib called. His immune system continues to drop. He's worried about his mother and about Greg. He sees himself as dying and Greg as living.

July 17, 1986

I went out to lunch with two of my friends, and I expressed my worry. Ann leaned over to me and said, "They both have AIDS, Carolyn. You will have to accept that." I didn't like hearing these words, and I wished I had just stayed home. But I knew what she said was true. What I had been afraid of, I could no longer deny. From this moment on, life would never be as secure.

Everyone is frightened about the virus. Some people are saying that gay men deserve this virus because they are gay. Greg lives in silence about his and Nagib's situation. And often so must I. I cannot share my fear with any assurance that anyone will care. I have mentioned it at work and have been met with a cold silence and then a change of subject.

I am angry at some of the talk I hear. The idea that some people are innocent victims while others are guilty is abhorrent to me. Don't people understand that this is a killing virus, that sex is a biological demand whether we are homosexual or heterosexual, and that all sexually active people are at risk.

August 26, 1986

Nagib has shingles, the first overt physical symptom that either one of them has had.

August 27, 1986

Sometimes in the depth of my soul I feel responsible that Greg is in jeopardy. If only I had given him enough good feelings about being gay, perhaps he would have been more careful.

October 31, 1986

Last night I said to Rod, "It's important that we talk about Greg. Nobody cares as much as we do." We cried together.

Internally, I'm walking a fine line as I try to come to terms with this situation. I don't want to dwell on the tragedy of this disease. I don't want to deny the problem. I want to be prepared for the worst, yet I don't want to go through pain until I have to.

Staying focused on what is important to me helps. I know how much I love my children. They're fun. They, to a minor extent, represent me. They contribute to my mental health and to my strength. What will happen if one of them dies before I do? Will I disappear? Will I still be important? Will I still have a purpose in life? Will I still enjoy my life?

"Stop it, Carolyn," I say to myself. "You are hurting. But you will survive."

November 10, 1988

Yesterday Millie and I had lunch together at the Galleria. She knew that her son was positive a year before we knew about Greg and Nagib. From the very first she and I have talked together about our innermost feelings and fears. We call each other for comfort and information. But yesterday we both voiced thoughts that we had never shared with anyone. The most troublesome idea that we spoke of was what we would do if either of our sons' quality of life became so miserable that they would choose to kill themselves. Would we assist them? Could we stand watching a son die? We sat there for hours and finally decided that we'd do what they asked. I know this sounds crazy, but I felt better.

Close friends have been by my side throughout this whole ordeal. Marian goes to lunch with me and listens and listens and listens. When I'm afraid that I've been talking too much, I look in her eyes and see compassion for me. This allows me to have compassion for myself, something I have trouble with.

My other friends make time for me and encourage me to share my concerns. Each friend gives me a special kind of support, and between them all I feel nutured. They have helped me get a grip on my feelings and make good decisions on what kinds of things I am able and need to do. This includes doing what is good for me and Rod and Stan and Robin, as well as for Greg.

December 1, 1986

Nagib has been diagnosed with AIDS-related complex (ARC), the phase of this disease where his helper cells begin losing ground. His immune system has not recovered from his bout with shingles. My feelings withdraw as another step is taken toward his death and toward Greg's.

December 10, 1986

Last night I cried over Greg and Nagib. Greg's troubles pull me toward him, and my maternal behaviors come creeping back. I know that I have no control over Greg and his illness. I need to let go, but his having HIV makes it hard. The virus interferes with my inner success at letting him go. Instead of sitting back and watching how he lives his life, I am back to wondering what is the best way to treat him.

The Disease Progresses

January 2, 1987

Greg and Nagib are leaving here today after a pretty good holiday. Yet Nagib had a high fever and was hard to get along with. More than once Greg asked me to try to comfort him. Nagib let me.

I think that feeling responsible for someone being ill must be a way to give control to the caregiver when in reality there is no control. Over and over, I have heard others speak of this desire for responsibility. Over and over, I have seen it turn against the person who either is anticipating the death of a loved one or who is in bereavement. This sense of guilt becomes particularly toxic for parents who have to watch their children die. I have to fight to keep from being bewildered and defeated by my self-generated guilt.

I say to myself now, "You are not the reason Greg is in danger. His being gay didn't cause him to get the virus. He was at the wrong place at the wrong time. He is strong and is taking good care of himself. You helped him to be an independent and capable man."

February 19, 1987

My panic and guilt about Greg have retreated into a safe place. I've spent much of the last few weeks thinking about the guilt issue and reassuring myself. I shall continue to do so today. It is helping me to put aside my obsessive thoughts and allows me to enjoy my life, at least for the time being.

February 26, 1987

AIDS is on my mind constantly today. I think again of my feeling of helplessness. It comes and goes with alarming frequency. When I haven't seen Greg and Nagib for a while, I manage to focus on my daily activities and keep the severity of their situation at bay. But when I finally get to be with them, my heart sinks and I can barely hold back my emotions.

March 30, 1987

We talked with Greg yesterday. His birthday had been on March 24th. He is twenty-nine and excited because of his success at work. His energy is not what it was, which he attributes to being overweight. His cholesterol is up and he drinks too much.

We told Greg last night how glad we were to have had him for twenty-nine years; that he enriched us.

If Greg dies before we do, our world will be turned upside down. What comforts me when these thoughts crowd into my mind is our current relationship.

April 28, 1987

Nagib called last night in a desperate state. I can only listen and care. I've decided not to suggest solutions, but only to do what he asks. His and Greg's options are slowly becoming fewer and fewer.

May 11, 1987

Yesterday was Mother's Day. Greg and Nagib called. Both of them haven't been feeling well. It took me until this morning to realize that I had anaesthesized myself. A steamroller approaches and I can't stop it. It hasn't hit yet. Something may divert it. There is hope. All is not over for Nagib or Greg.

May 12, 1987

I'm very worried about Nagib. I don't want to lose him.

June 22, 1987

Rod's dad is here, and Greg came home to see him. Greg is drinking a lot and appears anxious. I had asked Greg earlier in the day if he was feeling okay. "Mother, don't keep asking. It's upsetting me. I put my fear aside and then you bring it up." I agreed, but I felt cut off. Desperately I asked him to keep me informed of any changes, plus or minus. He then asked that Rod and I visit him as often as we can. That's a first. For some years Greg has pulled away from us. Now he's moving toward us. I force myself to honor his request to not ask too many questions. I will not hover.

June 29, 1987

It occurred to me yesterday that our lives are like an Alfred Hitchcock movie. The tension builds about whether Greg and Nagib will survive. Rod and I are helpless as we watch the scenarios develop. We try to put it aside, but the tension remains.

July 9, 1987

We've been to California to see Greg and Nagib. I perceived again an underlying anger from Greg toward Rod and me. Then it occurred to me that neither Rod nor I had accepted Greg as a gay little boy when he was growing up. During his whole childhood we had tried to develop his athletic skills in order to help him socially. Greg didn't fit our concept of how a boy should behave. When Greg rejected participating in boy activities, we turned to our "normal" son. We love Greg and Stan, but we approved of Stan more. This approval was subtle, but all of us knew it, and none of us talked about it.

We blundered on, thinking we were doing the right thing. In the process we managed to hurt both sons. Stan felt he had to be a super boy, and Greg felt he was a failure in his Dad's and my eyes. He thought we appreciated his abilities and achievements, but that somehow his "being" was not acceptable.

I do not say this to beat up on Rod and me. We were wrong in this part of our child raising. We were right in many others.

When I shared my insight with Rod, he agreed with what I thought. We decided to talk with Greg about what we had done. Greg was surprised when we apologized for how we contributed to his pain as a child. We made no excuses. Granted there were reasons, understandable from our point of view, but not from his. Greg was very warm to us the rest of the visit. His underlying anger and disappointment were lessened.

For years we've felt guilty about Greg, but we didn't know why. It has been constructive to know how and why Greg was hurt. Now, Rod and I are free of this underlying, unknown guilt, and Greg can let go of some of his pain from his childhood.

November 2, 1987

Greg sees no long-term future for himself. He's living as fully as he can each day. He's on AZT, a powerful antiviral.

November 29, 1987

Greg may be put in an experimental group to test another antiviral drug. I worry. The AZT helps. I don't know about this new one.

November 30, 1987

The virus is too active in Greg's bloodstream. He's not eligible to take part in the study.

February 23, 1988

Greg's blood is showing a reaction to AZT. He and Nagib are talking of separating. I felt good about their having each other for support, and now both of them are feeling very alone.

March 8, 1988

Greg's blood has picked up. He will be able to continue on the antiviral. He and Nagib are feeling hopeful about using the polio vaccine as a treatment. They are still together.

March 20, 1988

Lately not too much has been happening. I've calmed down and my life goes on as usual, except that I think about Greg a lot. I build scenarios in my head. Sometimes I see him dead. Sometimes I see myself caring for him as he gets sicker. Sometimes I wonder what I'll do with his things.

March 29, 1988

We arrived in L.A. two nights ago, looking forward to seeing Greg and Nagib. Getting there was easy, almost textbook-like in that everything went fine. But the moment we actually walked in at 11:00 P.M., the problems started for us and right now I am feeling overwhelmed.

Greg and Nagib told us they had argued most of the day. Much that was said was cruel and hurtful. They both said their relationship was over. Shortly after we arrived, Nagib rushed out and barely spoke to us. Greg, Rod, and I sat down and tried to make some sense out of what was happening. All of us were worried about Nagib. His behavior was totally unlike anything we had ever seen from him.

Greg then talked about himself. He said that this was the worst time of his life: losing Nagib, being in deep financial trouble, and having the AIDS-Related Complex himself. He thinks some of Nagib's reactions could be neurological, but that there was nothing he could do. Greg also said that the stress was bad for him and that he had to take care of himself. Rod and I just listened. We couldn't even offer financial support. Our limited resources would only block his financial problems temporarily and leave us without any cushion for an emergency. But Rod and I felt grateful and honored that Greg felt free enough to share so honestly with us.

Later on, after we finally had dinner, we continued our talking. Rod asked Greg how he was feeling. Greg said, "I'm dying. I may have five years or six months."

Rod said, "I know that must frighten you."

I sat and listened.

Greg answered, "No, I'm not frightened. I'm sad. It feels sad because I won't get to do all the things I've planned to do. I won't get to experience all that I wanted to."

Rod leaned over and touched him. I, being too far away to touch him, just leaned toward him. The three of us sat silent for a while, filled with sadness and love. After a long moment, Greg said, "I thought of turning to religion, but I can't believe there's anything after this. There's no life after death. There's just now."

He glanced at me and then at Rod. Seeing the pain in our eyes, he said, "It's not the end of the world." Rod and I were taken aback by his remark. He smiled and then said, "Well, for me it is." And we laughed gently about his trying to make light of the whole situation.

Later the conversation turned serious for him again. He said, "The only thing that could be worse for me is if I get full-blown AIDS or for either one of you to die. I don't think I could bear that. Please take care of yourselves." These words have been with me ever since.

With all our imperfections we are a family in the deepest sense of the word. Our roles are vague these days. The old ideas we lived by continue to be swept away, but the bonds that sustain us grow stronger.

Later on that evening Nagib came back. He looked strained and said his sight was getting worse. He hugged both Rod and me and said, "I love you no matter what happens with Greg and me."

I said, "It's okay to part, but please stay friends. You need each other. You've had six good years. Your and Greg's stress level is astronomical."

Nagib then sat down next to Greg and touched him warmly. He also wrote Greg a check to help with the bills that both of them had incurred earlier. This was the Nagib I've known and loved. I think he sees death approaching and is trying to run as hard as he can.

He left the condominium, and we went to bed exhausted.

When we got up the next morning, we found that Nagib had

returned sometime during the night. He asked Rod to take him to the doctor, who immediately hospitalized him. His sight is almost gone in his left eye, and he may lose all his sight permanently.

March 30, 1988

Yesterday Rod and I stayed at the hospital for seven hours. Nagib introduced us as his parents.

Greg is somehow managing this with great kindness. Yet he takes some care of himself.

March 31, 1988

Last night Greg, Rod, and I were coming home from the hospital. Rod and I were discussing what the doctor had said about Nagib's condition. Greg suddenly screamed, "Please stop talking. I can't take anymore. Take me home." We were all silent, and when we got back to his home, Greg only wanted to go to bed. For a brief moment I was afraid that I had hurt Greg. Rod said that he thought Greg's shouting out his feelings was good for him. I decided that Rod was right, and I felt somewhat better.

April 7, 1988

We've returned from L.A. We've been to hell and back. We now know that Nagib has the cytomegalovirus (CMV) in his eyes. They call it retinitis. Nagib is out of the hospital with a permanent implant in his chest so that he can take medicine that may or may not hold the CMV in check. He will take the medicine as long as he lives.

Greg's blood chemistry has changed for the worse. His suppressor cells are up; his helper cells are down. I cried for thirty minutes when I learned this. Rod and I decided to call more frequently.

I feel angry with Reagan and all those government officials who ignored HIV. I hate that the radical right uses it to attack gays and lesbians. I hate that many of the mainline churches have been so silent. I see Greg as a victim of their prejudice and hate.

April 21, 1988

My dreams are filled with death.

We got a card from Nagib on Tuesday. It was beautiful and incredibly sad. His thoughts were loving. His writing was shaky and poorly constructed.

It just occurred to me. Rod and I are going to go through this twice.

Nagib had eye surgery last night in an attempt to help his eyesight. We do not yet know the outcome.

May 24, 1988

After a week of lying on his stomach and not moving his head, Nagib found out the surgery did not work. In fact, his sight has deteriorated further. I fear he will become totally blind. Right now the only hope that he has is that his eyes may be saved enough to let him see light and dark.

I try to imagine life without sight. Sometimes when I get up at night and I'm feeling my way around the room, I think what it must be like for Nagib all the time.

June 27, 1988

Greg called yesterday saying he was afraid he had hurt our feelings on Saturday when he had told us his T cell count had dropped over a hundred points. He had been irritable and withdrawn, and he could tell we were upset by the change in our voices. Right then our being upset was too much for him. He hung up quickly. We understood on Saturday what was happening to him, but it felt good for him to want to reassure us. He needs to feel some power in his life. To do this, he is numbing his fear and sadness. Our response to the bad news broke through his defenses, and right now he desperately needs them.

After his call we went to the Gay Rights Parade and marched. I went to bed last night exhausted and had a dream. Someone gave me a baby boy to care for. He was small and not thriving. I was worried about his having problems because he was different. I began caring for the baby, feeling that I could help. Once I was careless and almost dropped him. His head fell back sickeningly. "You've hurt him badly," a voice said.

"No, he's fine," I said. The baby got down and began to walk and talk and say surprising things. "You see," I said, "the baby is fine. I didn't hurt him."

"Oh yes you have," said the voice, a man's voice. "Just wait and see."

I woke with pain in my chest that persisted for several hours.

July 8, 1988

Yesterday I cried and was angry all day. I felt this way because it seems to me today that my family is not close. None of us can talk about one of us dying.

July 10, 1988

Greg's T cells have jumped up to over 800, close to normal. Unless the test is wrong, which all of us fear, this is marvelous news. Something could be working. I hesitate to become too hopeful.

July 11, 1988

One of my friends who works with AIDS patients says the T cell counts fluctuate when you have the HIV virus and that the high number of Greg's T cells only signifies that he feels better when they're high. Life has become a seesaw. We're up one day and down the next.

I will listen to Marilyn Horne. Music connects me with the good in life. It allows me a way to express feelings. It lightens my burdens. It quietens my mind.

August 9, 1988

We've been to Greg's and Nagib's. They both are getting something out of life. I often wonder how they can do that. They continue to experience enjoyment, involvement, and are committed to live until they die. A son should not have to teach his mother this lesson.

August 30, 1988

Rod and I have been to L.A. again. The TV show *Hour Magazine* paid our way. We appeared on the show and then got to see Greg and Nagib. I don't get to see them enough.

September 15, 1988

Nagib called last night. The cytomegalovirus continues to attack his eyes. He's going blind, and there is no help for him. Nagib told me he wanted to die rather than be blind. I spoke with Greg briefly; he cried some, the first time in a long time.

I'm sick. My head aches.

November 18, 1988

Nagib's mother, Fadwa, has come from the Middle East to help. Thank God! Nagib is totally blind now.

The Situation Worsens

February 6, 1989

Nagib is worse. Greg has bronchitis. Is the bronchitis AIDS related? This is a question I do not want to ask out loud. Thoughts about Greg and Nagib come to me regularly and unexpectedly. Greg wants us to visit as often as we can.

April 5, 1989

I shy away from thinking and feeling how afraid Greg and Nagib must be.

September 7, 1989

Greg gave me importance and status when he was born. If he dies, where will I be? And now I answer, "You'll be where you've always been—on your own two feet."

Nagib is very ill. He has fluid around his heart. I don't think he'll last until Christmas.

November 14, 1989

Nagib has TB now. He looks as if he had spent years in a concentration camp. The doctor gives him only weeks to live. Rod and I went to L.A. to say good-bye. Nagib's suffering was so intense that we thought death would be a friend to him.

Greg's T cells remain inconsistent. I feel hungry and depressed.

December 23, 1989

Last night I fell asleep on the couch and had a dream: The family was downstairs watching TV. I became aware that Greg was missing. I kept asking Robin, Stan, and Rod where Greg was. They paid no attention to my concerns, and then I began shouting, "One of my children is missing! Where is he? He's missing! Where is he?" I woke up to the dog sleeping at my feet and Rod watching TV. For a short time I could hardly move.

December 26, 1989

The family was together this Christmas except for Greg and Nagib. We tried to get excited about our gifts and our being together, but we knew that the gifts we purchased for Nagib would not be used. I got him audiotapes that he will never hear. Still he hangs on. What a spirit he has!

Greg is different. He's far less judgmental and far more vulnerable. He's quieter, watchful, and more involved. It's as though his life is very precious to him, and the people in his life as well.

My life seems so poignant—joyous but with a deep sense of tragedy. The feeling drifts over me and covers me. The joy is because I love my family so; the tragedy is that I am losing Greg and Nagib.

January 1, 1990

Nagib is dying. Perhaps he's already dead. Hour by hour he's getting weaker. He barely responds, is incontinent, can't swallow, and breathes as though "two babies cry inside his chest." Fadwa and Greg are stoic, resigned, and frightened.

I realized, when this last phase started, that I have been working at ways of keeping my grief in check. Now my defenses no longer work. I have a heavy heart that is agonizing over the loss of someone I love, Nagib.

I remember first knowing him in the summer of 1982 when in the flush of his and Greg's new relationship, we were introduced. To me he was always kind and was enthusiastic about my projects. He managed restaurants and loved for us to come into his place of business. He was brilliant and kept all kinds of information in his head. He absorbed new knowledge like a sponge.

During the last twenty-one months his blindness developed, and he started his final, agonizing walk. He chose to share himself with Rod and me on an even deeper level. We felt honored. The day his mother came to L.A. in November of 1988, Nagib called us in a panic when Greg left to pick her up. He knew she would have to face his blindness, gayness, and coming death from AIDS. I had met her once before, and I reassured him that she would accept him. And she did. She went up to him immediately and took him in her arms and lovingly took care of him for fourteen months. No parent could do more.

The calls and sharing from Nagib continued. Whatever he was feeling, he shared with us. He held very little back, saying he no longer had time for games. Sometimes in his grief he was irrational. Once in a state of total frustration, he decided he wanted to build a bedside table. He called Rod for help. Rod gave him precise instructions about the kind of wood and tools he would need, and only at the end of the conversation did Rod mention safety. Of course, the table was never built, but Rod's respect for Nagib's wishes and need to feel some control in the face of his blindness defused the stress of the situation.

Each time Nagib's health took a nosedive he seemed to make a rash decision. Once he changed doctors. Another time he dismissed his nurse. Sometimes he quit taking his medicine. At times he became quite difficult as he faced his death.

Nagib and I shared music. He gave me his copy of *Anything Goes* during our last visit with him, because he hadn't felt well enough to go to Tower Records, a tradition between him and me.

The first time I went to Tower Records with Nagib, he impulsively took my hand and held it. I envied his freedom of physical expression, and I felt warm and cared for. That perception has never left me.

Yesterday in our last telephone conversation I said, "I love you, doll."

"I love you too," he painfully answered.

January 2, 1990

Nagib died at 4:30 our time this morning.

January 3, 1990

I feel numb, but Rod and I still manage to lash out at each other. Now that Nagib is dead, our full focus turns to Greg's health. I miss Nagib terribly. Just knowing I won't ever hear his voice hurts. What's happening to my tears? They are gone. I feel deadened and I push away all thoughts of AIDS. We've had AIDS in our family for four and one-half years now.

My intestinal tract is feeling even if I am not. I eat too much— my efficient method of stuffing my feelings. Whenever I am under stress, I fall back into old behaviors that helped me deal with problems in the past. Right now I think this is okay. It's easier to worry about my weight than it is to be overwhelmed by AIDS.

Greg is grieving and did not want us to be with him right now. He wanted Robin, instead. My usual hypersensitivity did not kick in for long. I realize that he doesn't need parenting. He's afraid of the time coming when we will have to care for him. He needs to feel in charge as much as he can.

God, I feel jumbled as my mind dashes here and there. I'm having trouble focusing. I do not want to face the inevitability of death, mine or the deaths of the people I love. I do not want to face that I really only have choices in how I react to life; that I had and have no power over its vicissitudes. My grief comes in waves.

Living is priceless. Each day, each moment, is all that I have. I act and react, feel, and take in what each moment brings. That's all there is. Being in the present will be quite enough, I hope. The past and future are empty and unreal. Time, then, has no parameters for me. The small moments of today are what counts. I will try to enjoy my time now.

January 23, 1990

As my bereavement about Nagib begins to fade, my anticipatory grief about Greg moves into my daily life. Nagib's death makes the idea of Greg's death more real. This morning I feel my old enemy, guilt: guilt at my lack of power, guilt because I didn't accept Greg as a gay little boy, guilt because I can't make him well, guilt because I used him to make me feel important, guilt because I still want much from him, and guilt because I will probably live after he is gone.

February 5, 1990

Greg is fixing up his condo, making plans to buy a house, and figuring out what he will do as he gets sicker. He's afraid of losing his job. He wrote Robin a beautiful letter about his experiences with Nagib the last two years.

March 2, 1990

Greg wants us to take his dog, Maggie. I think he wants to leave us something cherished by him. I must not take on his pain, but it is hard not to.

March 7, 1990

Greg is keeping Maggie. She keeps him from feeling so lonely.

March 20, 1990

Fadwa, Nagib's mother, visited us in Saint Louis on her way back to Lebanon. Her visit was hard and easy, wonderful and horrible. We talked often of how Nagib suffered from AIDS and our fears about what Greg might have to go through. The two of us have shared our sons, and I will miss her. She goes back to a war-torn country with no son and no husband, but she carries herself well.

March 24, 1990

Today is Greg's birthday. He's thirty-two. He is distancing himself from both Rod and me, and that hurts. I've talked to some friends at Parents FLAG about this. They say he is trying to spare us hurt. I think they are right, and I also think he is preparing to leave us.

Right now in his life he is experiencing sadness, terror, and loneliness. As he did when he was a child, he keeps himself apart from painful feelings and experiences. It helped him then, and it helps him now. He is surviving his days as best he can. Sometimes we do not fit into his concerns.

A New Relationship

May 1, 1990

Greg has a new relationship with a man named Manny. It's been going on for a month or so. Greg said he has little time left and that since Manny also has HIV, the two of them decided to go into this new relationship quickly.

They are planning to come home and visit next month.

June 8, 1990

Greg and Manny have been here along with the rest of the family. We are all impressed with Manny. He is friendly and compassionate. He's very aware of all our feelings and is not afraid to share his with us. He helped found the PLUS seminars in L.A. PLUS stands for "Positive Living for Us." The seminars are held every two months and are designed to help people who find out they are HIV-positive. Manny is one of the organizers. He's getting Greg interested.

I don't believe I've ever seen Greg so happy. He and Manny entered their relationship with eyes open. Both of them know what to expect and have decided to live each day as fully as they can.

But even with my joy over this new relationship, I look to the future with foreboding. I do not know how much more time we have with Greg.

May 11, 1991

We met many of Greg and Manny's friends on our last trip to L.A. About half of them are HIV-positive, and Manny has talked them into helping with the PLUS seminars. One evening the group decided to go out with Rod and me to a Mexican restaurant. Rod had too many margaritas, and Greg decided to take him home. The two of them were very close that night as their roles were reversed.

The rest of the group and I went to a piano bar. As we listened to the music, we noticed a young man who was all alone and seemed very sad. Manny and I started talking to him. He told us his lover had just died of AIDS, that he was all alone, and that he was also HIV-positive. The rest of the group moved toward him and he was included. At the end of the evening all the guys gave me hugs and assured me that Manny and Greg would have plenty of support as the disease progressed. I felt comforted.

October 23, 1991

Greg and Manny bring out the best in each other. Neither of them gives up on a relationship problem they might be having. Both of them are powerful personalities. Yet they have the ability to let go of hurtful feelings and admit when they are wrong. They are in touch with each other's needs and wants. I have not yet figured out who gives the most. I don't think I ever will. Theirs is the most equal relationship I have ever seen. The whole family enjoys being with them.

March 9, 1992

We've been to L.A. to see Greg and Manny. They're doing well. I'm relaxing a bit. My weight is still a battle for me. A person I know who does social work with families of AIDS patients told me that often family members will gain weight as the person with HIV loses weight.

April 10, 1992

I'm having a bad time this evening. I only know it because I'm ravenous. Today I read the *Being Alive* newsletter that AIDS Project Los Angeles publishes. The newsletter is very specific about possible opportunistic infections. As I read the descriptions, I was filled with a deep sense of dread. I know I need to talk about what is happening to me, but I can't.

May 7, 1992

I'm on the board of Delta, a mental health agency for persons affected by HIV. Everyone except me is gay or lesbian. I've never been a part of a group that is as competent and loving as this board is. I feel completely comfortable. We argue on how to be more inclusive, and the ideas generated are excellent. I feel inadequate in the idea department, but everyone treats me as though what I think is valuable.

May 19, 1992

My life is very full, but my sense of impending loss is strong. When I'm with my friends at Parents FLAG I feel very much cared about, and my hunger feelings retreat.

The Disease Becomes Critical

June 21, 1992

Father's Day. Bad news. The HIV virus is attacking Manny more virulently. His T cell count is now 130. AZT is not working any longer.

Manny will have to quit his job. The diarrhea is taking its toll.

July 13, 1992

We're back from seeing Joseph Gregory Jablonsky, Robin and Mike's new son. My grandson cannot take Greg's place, but he shows me that my ability to love is not compromised. As I held the baby, my feelings of love became so intense that I cried. I realized then that neither AIDS, nor homophobia, nor AIDSphobia could diminish my ability to give and receive love.

August 23, 1992

Greg and Manny got married on August 21st. The minister talked about how they had decided to live their lives as fully as they possibly could. He included specifics: Greg is adding to his Ph.D. with a clinical degree and plans to spend the rest of his life working with others who have HIV. Manny continues his work with the PLUS seminars and is constantly helping those who are ill. The two of them have parties, take trips, go to the opera, and take an active part in the raising of Manny's niece and nephews. Greg says, "We will live until we die."

At the end of the minister's talk, Manny and Greg stood holding hands; each with a brother and sister by his side and their parents looking on. Both families showed full support. People who worked with Greg and Manny were there, as well as their doctors and their friends. Our son Stan said it was the most significant wedding he had ever seen.

September 28, 1992

Manny's T cells have been down to 37, though now they are back up in the 100s. Greg has problems with the combination of antivirals he is taking. His liver is affected and he is losing muscle mass.

October 7, 1992

I'm on the brink of something that feels important to my well-being. It's got something to do with letting go of the idea deep inside of me that I can control what happens; letting go of hanging on to that which is ended; letting go of my denial of loss.

I feel good about me, deeply and pridefully good—not better or best, just good. I'm grateful for that part of my personality which struggles and learns and accepts.

January 7, 1993

The holidays were good even in the midst of looking at my sister Martha's declining health as well as Greg and Manny's. All of them are weaker than they were last year. During the entire season I was able to enjoy the good moments. Greg and Stan were closer, mainly because Manny eases their sibling rivalry and resentments.

February 4, 1993

Martha died today. I'm on my knees. I can't read, write, or listen to music.

January 22, 1994

I've decided to start my journal again. Manny has Kaposi's sarcoma.

May 28, 1994

We were finally able to schedule a PLUS seminar with Greg and Manny. They were volunteers.

The seminar lasted the whole weekend and covered practical information, spiritual information, nutritional information, and medical information. We also had small groups where we shared our feelings and needs. There were 100 participants plus 50 volunteers, and even though the gay and lesbian community ran the weekend, all people affected by AIDS were welcomed.

At the closing ceremony the participants formed a large circle holding hands. The volunteers formed a smaller, inner circle facing the participants. A song, "That's What Friends Are For," began. As they walked the circle, each volunteer looked at each participant. When Greg and Manny passed me singing and smiling, I felt connected to them. It was one of the most spiritual activities I have ever participated in.

June 21, 1994

Manny is getting sicker. Soon he's going on a temporary IV feeding in an effort to slow down his weight loss.

Part of the AIDS quilt was in Saint Louis this week. One of my friends had made a quilt for Nagib. At first I didn't want to be reminded of Nagib's dying, but I felt that I would be letting him down if I didn't go. The quilt was shown at Washington University's Field House. When I walked in, I found a subdued room where people silently showed their respect. At first I could not find Nagib's quilt. Then I saw it. I stopped and stood there and images of Nagib came to me. I felt tears, but I made no sound. I took pictures to send to his mother and to Greg and then turned to leave. A friend of mine saw me and reached her arms out to me. Without speaking we wept.

July 18, 1994

We met Greg and Manny in Santa Fe for a vacation and had a fine time. Manny continues to lose ground and all of us were strained. Yet we enjoyed the opera, the shops, the museums, and the scenery.

The day we got home, Greg called to tell us he has hepatitis. We were stunned. He also told us he was going on permanent disability.

October 19, 1994

Much has happened. Stan and Laurie have a new daughter, and we have a new granddaughter, Sarah Jean. Manny continues to disintegrate, and Greg now has diabetes and has stopped drinking. I turn sixty this month, and I now admit to the very real possibility of my own death. All is not well.

January 2, 1995

A new year. Everyone says, "Happy New Year!" and I think, "Not for us." But I smile and eat and push aside the fear. It's a knowing, an awareness of how sick Manny is, and though Greg is not as sick as Manny, he is definitely not up to par. His T cells are going down; he was sick the whole time he was here at Christmas; he's on a new combination antiviral medicine.

Manny is fighting the cytomegalovirus, pneumonia, Kaposi's sarcoma, and intestinal problems. I figure he spends at least half of his waking hours dealing with medical issues. He's very irritable, and Greg gets most of his irritability. So Greg goes to the gym and works out for two or three hours each day. I numb out.

We talked to the guys about our coming to L.A. every two months or so. Both seemed genuinely receptive to our visiting this often. I don't want to be a nuisance, but I want to be with them as much as I can. So does Rod.

February 14, 1995

I have a plan to help me go through this with Greg and Manny. Feel and let go; feel and let go; understand and let go; problem solve and let go; repeat as often as necessary. God, I hope this helps.

March 2, 1995

Greg is a long-time survivor, but today his T cells are 230. When the T cell count gets down to 200, it is considered full-blown AIDS. For so long I have fooled myself that his getting seriously ill was far in the future. Today I don't feel that way.

Greg has a photographic memory. His reading level is such that he can read and understand the gobbledygook of corporate America, the fog index in most insurance forms, medical explanations, and what is found in most scientific journals. It's a chilling thought that he could get dementia and lose his mental ability.

March 15, 1995

Manny has been hospitalized with Pneumocystis pneumonia. He cannot tolerate the drug of choice. How much more can he stand?

March 24, 1995

Another birthday for Greg. He is thirty-seven years old. Rod and I are afraid and spaced out, worrying about his health. The only ways we can help him now are to fix broken things around his house or clean up for him. Both Greg and Manny are getting sicker and sicker. Watching them when we visit, and talking on the phone with them when we can't, leaves me weak because I don't know how and what to do. Sometimes I want to be Florence Nightingale, and then I think, "You're hovering." Sometimes I want to be a therapist with them, and then I think, "They're my children, not my clients." Sometimes I pretend that everything is just fine, and then I think, "Don't cut them off! Be there when *they* want and need you." As I watch their lives fade away, my inner child screams, "Don't go!" They smile sadly, but they go.

I am thankful that Greg has Manny. The two of them help each other more than anyone else can. The love that they share spills onto Rod and me, and somehow comforts us.

How many more birthdays can we celebrate with you, Greg? How many more birthdays will you and Manny have together?

March 30, 1995

I am very tired. I long to rest and refresh myself. Instead, I push on and my tiredness stays on a constant plane. I am tired when I wake; I am tired at night; I am tired all the time. Holding back my feelings takes an enormous effort. I have no relief from a bone-breaking fear.

July 17, 1995

Ten years have gone by since we started dealing with this disease. I've become used to the additional burden. As Greg and

Manny's health have gone down, my weight has gone up. Sometimes I am not aware of AIDS; sometimes it stays on my mind without letup. It cuts my energy in half, and my pleasures in life have become less. I stumble and fall, and then I pick myself up and try to understand. Greg and Manny help. They are strong men, and they do not want physical care by a parental figure. Rod says they will have no choice.

August 12, 1995

We received a letter from Fadwa, who said, "It's been five years and seven months since Nagib died, and it gets no easier for me." She has developed physical problems and is at a loss about what to do. Few people know that her son died from AIDS. She deals with her sadness alone, and it does not leave her. It's like she is on a treadmill of grief.

Greg had a severe headache while we were visiting in L.A. Manny's eyes are not doing well. They both are going to have brain scans.

Manny feels more and more helpless and acts more and more controlling. He is afraid of leaving his sister and her children and wants to teach them all that he knows. The children cannot understand his desperate attempts to make sure they act "correctly."

Manny has decided to quit fighting if his quality of life becomes such that he is miserable all the time. Over and over, he has asked me to support him and Greg if he reaches that stage. I do, and so does Rod. One minute Greg and Manny talk about dying but then will immediately make long-term plans.

Greg and Manny hold each other when they are scared, stand up for each other, respect each other's needs, argue, support, and encourage each other as both of them are facing the most difficult issue any of us ever face, our own death.

August 15, 1995

Neither Greg's nor Manny's brain scans showed damage. We have a reprieve.

SUMMARY

The ten years that I have known that Greg was HIV-positive have been hard. It is confusing and heart-wrenching to have my child teach me about death. It goes against everything I expect. There are few institutional supports for those of us who are losing our loved ones to AIDS. Our family has fumbled through these years and has discovered some thoughts and beliefs that helped us. Perhaps they can help you.

- Each person grieves in her or his own way.
- All family members need support.
- The person with AIDS needs to make as many decisions as he or she possibly can.
- The gay and lesbian community has done a magnificent job dealing with the whole crisis.
- Expressing feelings in some way seems to be helpful for the persons living with AIDS and for the people who love and support them.
- Hope is followed by disappointment, followed by hope, followed by disappointment, followed by hope. This appears to me to be the nature of this disease. Our family has learned to live with this yo-yo existence.
- Facing death often creates an unconditional appreciation of life.
- The sanctity of gay relationships, really all relationships, deserves our utmost respect.
- We are grateful that our son is a member of the gay community. The help that he has received from his community is immeasurable. Social support has made his and our journey easier.
- Our family is very proud of the way our son has handled himself throughout his adult life. He is strong and a fighter. His ability to attack the problem and stay hopeful has enhanced his life and ours.

- Being informed gives more choices. The more the choices were acted on, the better were our physical and emotional conditions. Our son and his partner tried acupuncture, chiropractic, antivirals, individual and group counseling, and all available medical treatment. They are aware of the latest medical and drug research and will seek out ways to get the drugs or new treatments. They also understand their insurance systems and what kinds of services are available.
- The more we contacted and supported others, the more we helped ourselves.
- Books, books, books. (See the Bibliography.)
- Keeping a journal.
- We recognize that when the AIDS situation deteriorates, our irritability level increases.
- We don't have to deal with AIDS all the time.

AFTERWORD

from GREGORY M. GRIFFIN

Often I think children of a certain age are so involved in becoming adults and establishing their own lives that they neglect to consider the changes and growth, love and support, of their families. I plead guilty to the above and thus I am grateful to have been given this opportunity to remark about two rather extraordinary people, my mom and dad.

I struggled, cried, and despaired about my own emerging sexuality from before I was twelve years old until I was almost eigh-

Gregory M. Griffin, Ph.D., is a mathematical psychologist.

teen. At that point, while still in high school, I rather grandiosely informed my parents that I was a homosexual and dating a man eighteen years my senior. That was a very difficult decision for me, but somehow in my naïveté, or rather innocence, I thought that having told them the "facts" of the matter, the issues would immediately be resolved. It took much longer. I ignored the time that it took me to come to the first steps of accepting myself. I ignored my parents' expectations of grandchildren and the traditional extended familial relationships that they were anticipating. But I did not forget how much they loved me—a fact that probably made things more difficult for them.

I never doubted my parents. I never thought for a minute they would cut off our relationship. I never thought that they would not come to respect and understand me as a gay man. And they have.

There is a lot of lip service paid these days to family values. Many associate these values—love, support, loyalty, integrity, morality, stability—only with traditional families. These values need no defense, nor does the traditional family. But an alternative family or lifestyle does not preclude having those values. I'm pretty lucky in this area with my own family.

I think this book may bring families closer together, and maybe even make a real difference in some people's lives. I hope knowing this gives my mom and dad the joy and pride they deserve. Thanks, Mom and Dad.

AFTERWORD

from SCOTT WIRTH

For the gay nature that lay behind the vision and trouble that bore this book, I give thanks. To my mother and father, for their journey and for their love, I give thanks.

My parents and I took the opportunity to make the truth of who we were the priority of our adult relationship. In opening ourselves, we have come to see and largely heal the rifts that separated us in the years of my childhood and adolescence.

Scott Wirth, Ph.D., is a psychologist and consultant in private practice in San Francisco, California.

Gay people may recognize the sources of such missed connections: A young father's need for his son to be an image of himself that the son does not fulfill; then the wounded son's withdrawal from the disappointed father; a mother's sensing her son as "different," and encouraging him to be so in the "safer" ways—"He is musical." She shrinks back from her intuitions about him in order to be an "appropriate" mother. Both parents become fascinated and bewildered by their son's "sensitivity," by his disregard for gender-typed interests, by their own feelings that there is something indefinably "wrong" about themselves or him, by their feelings of being depressed, mute, or angry. This son, as a teenager, numbing his sexual being for lack of role models or validation; finding no approving gleam in his parents' eyes, and no response from his peers' experiences.

He and they cannot sort out whether the "differentness" lies in his true self or in his "problems." What is this differentness anyhow? "It" is vague, a threatening whisper in the mind, not to be reinforced. Out of the helplessness of not knowing, come the clichés: "It will pass—it's just a phase—he's sensitive—we do the best we can." Even living beneath the same roof, they inadvertently misconstrue each other.

But this misunderstanding was not simply an isolated family matter. There was no room in society for gay and lesbian children or youth. The McCarthyist society of the fifties and early sixties was systematically hostile to racial and ethnic minorities, women, and political dissidents as well as to gay people—in fact, to anyone other than prosperous heterosexual white males.

Beyond Acceptance makes it plain that adult gay children and their parents need not protect each other from telling their stories. Raising my parents' consciousness also meant sensitizing them—to themselves, to each other, to "modern times." In the early stages, this effort felt burdensome to me. I felt that I shouldn't have had to do all that work. At different times I felt indignant, trapped, resigned, or lost for having to, in a sense, parent my parents.

Yet, what once seemed an undue imposition has evolved into a mutual process of joyful struggle and deepening intimacy. This newfound honesty led us not only back to each other, but out into the world of human service—for myself as a psychologist and community activist—for my parents as authors and Parents FLAG organizers.

Service often comes best out of work on ourselves. And in this work on ourselves, as is said in Zen, "The greater the hindrance, the greater the enlightenment." Sharing this philosophy with each other, we came to know our "enlightenment" as a process that includes setbacks. There is an inevitable return to the edge of frustration or discouragement. Whatever that edge may be, we can meet it with patience. That patience will see us through our resistance to change.

For some parents, growth may mean going beyond a virtuous or martyred I-accept-my-child stance. For some lesbians and gay men, personal growth may mean accepting the nonacceptance of parents and siblings and finding a self-love within. Whether we are challenging and confronting, or letting go and letting be, what seems needed is an openness to the unexpected.

Gayness or lesbianism presents itself in our lives unexpectedly. It goes on to surprise us, to confuse us, to disappear and reappear, to open us. Just about the time we think we truly affirm the dignity of gay people, we may feel like Judas Iscariot as we let an ignorant comment or joke breeze through a conversation. Just as we find our comfortable orientation number on the Kinsey scale, we experience feelings or fantasies at the other end of the spectrum. Right after a lecture against stereotypes of gay people, someone walks in who seems to fit them all. Grandchildren may be born to the lesbian daughter or gay son for whom a parent had ruled out the possibility. After working through our phobic attitudes about the sexual part of homosexuality, we hear that gay people resent an overemphasis on sex in gay relationships. The very designation "gay" may seem a liberating affirmation of identity in one moment, then a simple, utterly dehumanizing label in the next.

Being gay, or closely related to someone who is, offers an uncommonly powerful catalyst for personal transformation. If we can stand the heat and give ourselves over to the full scope of the process of coming out, we will learn flexibility in the midst of life's chaos, paradox, and mystery.

APPENDIX

Parents, Families and Friends of Lesbians and Gays (P-FLAG) is a nonsectarian, nonprofit national and international organization. Its purpose is to help parents so that they can help themselves and their lesbian and gay children.

P-FLAG affiliates are located in more than 400 communities in all fifty states, the District of Columbia, Puerto Rico, and ten other countries.

To find a group or groups near you, call or write the national office. The staff and volunteers will help you with complete confidentiality.

The address for P-FLAG is:

> P-FLAG
> 1101 14th St. N.W., Suite 1030
> Washington, DC 20005
>
> Telephone: (202) 638-4200
> Fax: (202) 638-0243
> E-mail: PFLAGNTL@AOL.COM

What is it like at a P-FLAG meeting? There is no fee, no pressure to say or do anything. You may wish to just listen at first. You may use your first name only. Confidentiality is assured. You will find friendly, informed parents who understand your feelings because they have been there themselves.

BIBLIOGRAPHY

A more detailed *Recommended Reading List,* as well as a list of P-FLAG publications, is available from:

> Parents, Families and Friends of Lesbians and Gays
> 1101 14th St., N.W., Suite 1030
> Washington, DC 20005
> Telephone: (202) 638-4200
> Fax: (202) 638-0243
> E-mail: PFLAGNTL@AOL.COM

GENERAL

Aarons, Leroy. *Prayers for Bobby: A Mother's Coming to Terms with the Suicide of Her Gay Son.* San Francisco: HarperCollins, 1995.

Bell, Alan P., Martin S. Weinberg, and Sue K. Hammersmith. *Sexual Preference: Its Development in Men and Women.* Bloomington: Indiana University Press, 1981.

Bernstein, Robert A. *Straight Parents, Gay Children: Keeping Families Together.* New York: Thunder's Mouth Press, 1995.

Borhek, Mary V. *My Son Eric.* New York: The Pilgrim Press, 1979.

Burr, Chandler. *A Separate Creation: The Search for the Biological Origins of Sexual Orientation.* New York: Hyperion, 1996.

Buxton, Amity Pierce. *The Other Side of the Closet.* Santa Monica: IBS Press, 1991. For spouses of gays.

Clark, Don. *Loving Someone Gay,* revised and updated. Millbrae, Conn.: Celestial Arts Publications, 1987.

Cole, Beverly. *Cleaning Closets: A Mother's Story.* Saint Louis: Chalice Press, 1996.

Dew, Robb Forman. *The Family Heart: A Memoir of When Our Son Came Out.* Reading, Mass.: Addison-Wesley, 1994. Also available on audio tape from Simon and Schuster.

Fairchild, Betty, and Nancy Hayward. *Now That You Know: What Every Parent Should Know About Homosexuality.* New York: Harcourt Brace Jovanovich, 1989.

Heron, Ann., ed. *Two Teenagers in Twenty.* Boston: Alyson Publications, 1994.

Jennings, Kevin, ed. *Becoming Visible: A Reader in Gay and Lesbian History for High School and College Students.* Boston: Alyson Publications, 1994.

Marcus, Eric. *Is It a Choice? Answers to 300 of the Most Frequently Asked Questions About Gays and Lesbians.* San Francisco: HarperSanFrancisco, 1993.

McNaught, Brian. *On Being Gay: Thoughts on Family, Faith, and Love.* New York: St. Martin's Press, 1988.

Mondimore, Francis D. *Understanding Homosexuality.* Baltimore: Johns Hopkins University Press, 1994. Current biological and psychiatric research.

Monette, Paul. *Becoming a Man: Half a Life Story.* San Francisco: HarperCollins, 1992.

P-FLAG. *Why Ask Why? Addressing the Research on Homosexuality and Biology.* Washington, D.C.: P-FLAG, 1995.

Price, Deb, and Joyce Murdock. *And Say Hi to Joyce: America's First Gay Column Comes Out.* Garden City, N.Y.: Doubleday, 1995.

Rafkin, Louise. *Different Daughters: A Book by Mothers of Lesbians.* Pittsburgh and San Francisco: Cleis Press, 1987.

Sherman, Phillip. *Uncommon Heroes: A Celebration of Heroes and Role Models for Gay and Lesbian Americans.* New York: Fletcher Press, 1994.

Shyer, Marlene Fanta, and Chris Shyer. *Not Like Other Boys: Growing Up Gay— A Mother and Son Look Back.* Boston: Houghton Mifflin, 1996.

Williams, Walter L. *The Spirit and the Flesh: Sexual Diversity in American Indian Culture.* Boston: Beacon Press, 1986.

RELIGION AND HOMOSEXUALITY

Balka, Christie, and Andy Rose. *Twice Blessed: On Being Lesbian and Gay and Jewish.* Boston: Beacon Press, 1989.

Gramick, Jeannine, and Robert Nugent, eds. *Voices of Hope: A Collection of Positive Catholic Writings on Gay and Lesbian Issues.* Mount Ranier, Md.: New Ways Ministry, 1995.

Nugent, Robert, and Jeannine Gramick. *Building Bridges: Gay and Lesbian Reality and the Catholic Church.* Boston: Beacon Press, 1995.

Scanzoni, Letha, and Virginia R. Mollenkott. *Is the Homosexual My Neighbor?* San Francisco: Harper and Row, 1978.

White, Mel. *Stranger at the Gate.* New York: Simon and Schuster, 1994.

HIV/AIDS

Nuland, Sherwin B. *How We Die.* New York: Alfred A. Knopf, 1994.

Pohl, Mel, Kay Deniston, and Doug Toft. *The Caregivers' Journey.* Center City, Minn.: Hazelden Foundation, 1990.

Shilts, Randy. *And the Band Played On: Politics, People, and the AIDS Epidemic.* New York: Penguin Books, 1988.

Veninga, Robert A. *A Gift of Hope: How We Survive Our Tragedies.* New York: Ballantine Books, 1988.

Verghese, Abraham. *My Own Country.* New York: Random House, 1995.

INDEX